Russia and

Russia and the Media

The Makings of a New Cold War

Greg McLaughlin

First published 2020 by Pluto Press
345 Archway Road, London N6 5AA

www.plutobooks.com

Copyright © Greg McLaughlin 2020

'Di Eagle an Di Bear' by Linton Kwesi Johnson © LKJ Records Ltd/LKJ Music
Publishers Ltd; reproduced by permission.

The right of Greg McLaughlin to be identified as the author of this work has
been asserted by him in accordance with the Copyright, Designs and Patents
Act 1988.

British Library Cataloguing in Publication Data
A catalogue record for this book is available from the British Library

ISBN   978 0 7453 3767 8   Hardback
ISBN   978 0 7453 3765 4   Paperback
ISBN   978 1 7868 0523 2   PDF eBook
ISBN   978 1 7868 0525 6   Kindle eBook
ISBN   978 1 7868 0524 9   EPUB eBook

This book is printed on paper suitable for recycling and made from fully
managed and sustained forest sources. Logging, pulping and manufacturing
processes are expected to conform to the environmental standards of the
country of origin.

Typeset by Stanford DTP Services, Northampton, England

Simultaneously printed in the United Kingdom and United States of America

To my Sue with love

And in memory of my Mum, Maureen (1930–2017)

Contents

Acknowledgements

I want to offer my warm thanks and appreciation here to the people who helped me see this book through to completion and into production.

At Pluto Press, commissioning editor, David Castle, for his priceless patience and wise counsel, especially during personal difficulty with the passing of my mother; managing editor, Robert Webb, for his expert supervision of the book's production; copy editor Thérèse Wassily Saba for her guidance and advice; and typesetter, Dave Stanford; and Melanie Patrick and her colleagues, Emily Orford, Kieran O'Connor, Chris Browne and William Confalone for their superb cover design and promotional work.

Thanks also to Mary Dejevsky, former Russia correspondent and now special correspondent on China and Europe with the *Guardian*, for giving me her valuable time and expertise for an excellent interview; and to the musician and dub poet, Linton Kwesi Johnson, for allowing me to reproduce in full his song, 'Di Eagle and Di Bear'.

On a personal level, thanks to my friends and former colleagues, David Butler, Stephen Baker and Colm Murphy, for their advice and support along the way; to my wife, Sue, for reading draft chapters and pointing out what should have been obvious mistakes; to her two boys, Jake and Sam, and to my brothers and sisters and their families for their support and encouragement.

A chéad míle buíochas le gach

Di Eagle an Di Bear

Di Eagle and di Bear a keep a living in fear
Of the impending nuclear warfare
But as a matter of fact, believe it or not
Plenty people don't care whether it imminent or not
Or who di first one to attack or if the human race
[aba] survive or not
For those whom is aware
Them life already coming like a nightmare

And you can see it everywhere
The famine and the fear
The doubt and the drought
Desperation and despair
And you can see it all around
The massacres abound
Dead bodies all around
The atrocities abound
Missing persons can't be found
Dictators get dethroned
New clowns are quickly found

© Linton Kwesi Johnson, 1983

Preface
The Cold War And Me

Linton Kwesi Johnson's poem, 'Di Eagle and Di Bear', laments the insanity and instability generated by the politics and propaganda of the Cold War of the 1980s. But it also makes a distinction between those who did not care, and got on with their lives, and those who did care and whose lives were 'already coming like a nightmare'. I was in my late teens/early twenties during that decade and my response to the threat of a nuclear apocalypse was to seek safety in books. Books about nuclear weapons and what they did to people. Books about Hiroshima and Nagasaki. Books about the superpowers, the USA and the Soviet Union, and their deadly rivalry. Books about freedom and democracy and communism and totalitarianism, and what those words meant or were supposed to mean. Books about communism and how evil it was. Then I started reading about alternatives. Books about Che Guevara and the revolutions of Africa and Central and South America. Books about American corporations and right-wing death squads in Managua and San Salvador and Lima and Buenos Aires. Books about Cuba and Angola. Far too many books and too much confusion, one would think, for a wee boy living in Derry, in the war-torn north of Ireland. But I kept reading anyway because I could get no sense from any other source of this bigger, global war that was 'cold' but could blow up at any time and destroy us all. It was all so scary, yet strangely abstract. The local librarian must have been concerned.

Then I took a degree in Media Studies at university and there it was again. The Cold War. This time, though, I was reading books about media reporting of the Cold War, about the propaganda and the relationship between the two. I even based my dissertation on the question. It was called, 'News from the Evil Empire', and it looked at reporting of this 'seminal moment' in the conflict: the Moscow

Summit between US president Ronald Reagan and Soviet president, Mikhail Gorbachev, in 1988. Things seemed to be changing. The images and the rhetoric of this war of ideologies were softening and so was the media reporting.

Until that point, I had no ambitions to go any further than graduation but I was hooked. When I graduated in the following year, 1989, I went to Glasgow University to start a PhD on the changing images of the Soviet Union. The East European revolutions were happening and the Berlin Wall came down, one of the most iconic symbols of Cold War division. By the end of 1991, Germany was reunited and the Soviet Union ceased to exist. The Cold War was history and, to evoke Stanley Kubrick's satirical film, *Dr Strangelove*, people stopped worrying about the bomb. Yet the language and imagery of the Cold War did not go away. In less than ten years, the media had identified a new enemy to watch: Vladimir Putin, President of Russia. It has been impossible for me to resist the question: what, if anything, has changed since the Cold War?

1

Introduction

Love, friendship and respect do not unite people as much as a common hatred for something
(Notebook of Anton Chekov, 1987)[1]

What do we in 'the West' know about Russia? Do we know that it is the largest country in the world, with a surface area of over 17.1 million square kilometres, with 11 time zones, west to east, and with a diverse population, in terms of ethnicity and language, of 144 million? Do we know of its vast natural resources on which we are dependent? Do we know of its rich, artistic heritage – its literature, its music, its art and its cinema? Do we know of its long, turbulent history from the first century AD through to the ascendancy of the Tsars in the early seventeenth century and the emergence of the Russian Empire a century later? Do we know much about the Russian revolutions that brought radical change to the country in 1917 and, in the words of the American journalist, John Reid, 'shook the world' into a new way of thinking about Russia's political axis? No longer isolationist but internationalist and, arguably, more confrontational?

Gradually, the great divide in the world became less about different empires and alliances than between Russia, with its revolutionary ideas of Marxism and Communism, and the West and its twin ideologies of capitalism and liberal democracy. How much do we know about the history of mutual suspicion, mistrust and even hatred that marked the relationship between Russia and what developed into the greater Soviet Union (East) and us (West)? Do we know about the horrors of forced migrations and the collectivisation of farmland in the Soviet Union of the 1930s? Or the role of the Soviet Union in the Second World War, once it became an ally of the West, in winning the war against Adolf Hitler's Nazi regime in Germany? Do we know that the Soviet death toll in that war, of over 20 million people, civilians and military, far exceeded that of the rest of the Western allies, combined? Do we know about the nuclear bombing by the USA of Hiroshima and Nagasaki, with a combined death toll of anything between 120,000 to 220,000 human souls, depending how one counts? Do we know about the nuclear arms race between the West and the Soviet Union? About the hardening of the divide between us? The Iron Curtain? The Berlin Wall? The Cuban Missile crisis? And the various other misunderstandings, accidents and near misses that could have ended it all, for all of us? Do we remember those television documentaries about what would happen in the event of a nuclear strike, or the public information advertisements advising people that, in the event of an incoming nuclear missile strike, we should hide behind a sandbag, close one's eyes and hope (in our dying seconds) that everything would work out fine?

Then again, do we know about the days of hope? The 1980s and the arrival of a new leader of the Soviet Union, Mikhail Gorbachev ('Gorby') and his visits to the West? How he transformed the ways in which Western publics saw the Soviet Union, or the 'Evil Empire' as US President Ronald Reagan called it? Do we know about the revolutions that spread throughout Eastern Europe in 1989? The symbolic 'Fall of the Berlin Wall' in November of that year? And do we know or remember that on 25 December 1991, the red flag of the Soviet Union with its hammer and sickle, the symbol of the union of workers and peasants, was lowered on the Kremlin, Moscow, for the very last time? The Soviet Union was no more. The Cold War was over; the West was triumphant. But there was still a Russia and it entered into a decade of immense social, political and economic chaos. This was illuminated in many ways by the personality and style of the first president of the new Russian republic, Boris Yeltsin. In the space of two four-year terms, beginning in June 1991, he oversaw the transformation of Russia from a Stalinist command and control state to being a free market republic along Western lines. Yet he also oversaw the catastrophic transfer of wealth from the state into private hands – most worryingly in the oil, mineral, industrial and financial sectors – and the impoverishment of a large section of the population. However, Yeltsin did not see out the whole of his second term as president. Increasingly unable to function in office due to ill health and alcoholism, he resigned on 31 December 1999, and was replaced on an interim basis by his prime minister, Vladimir S. Putin. Within three months, Putin prevailed against a divided and chaotic bloc of opposition parties – nationalists, communists and Western-facing liberals – to get elected as president of Russia on a majority of 52 per cent of the electorate. He was re-elected in 2004 but gave way constitutionally, in 2008, to a new candidate, Dmitry Medvedev, on the understanding that the new president would not run against him in the next contest, scheduled for 2012. In the interim period, the new administration approved an extension of the presidential term from four to six years, starting from 2012, allowing Putin to run for and win that new term and another renewed mandate in 2018. By the time that comes to a close, in 2024, Vladimir Putin will have been the effective ruler of Russia for 25 years. Whether he formally gives up power for good at that point is uncertain. He will be 72 years old and perhaps looking forward at that point to a long and happy retirement in the holiday resort of Sochi? Or perhaps he will find a way to extend his rule for another term?

In the 20 years he has been in power, Putin has emerged as a relatively powerful politician at home and abroad. He has used the chaos of domestic politics to establish himself as the only sensible choice for a people wanting sustainability in the economy and credibility in foreign affairs. He has presented himself as a strong man, a new Tsar Peter the Great, not afraid to face down the out-of-control oligarchs, who are widely blamed for the country's economic degradation. And he has not been afraid to face down the West and call their bluff, with their seeming determination to surround Russia and keep it locked down. This book will focus on the Western media image of Putin and Russia that emerged very quickly from the start of his first term as president in 2000.

STRUCTURE, METHOD AND MEDIA SAMPLES

At the heart of this book is a thematic analysis of how our media has responded to the rise of Putin to power, with reference to key moments in his relationship with the West: from the start of the Second Chechen War, in 1999, to early 2019. The book begins, in Chapter 2, by setting the analysis in historical context, reviewing the role the Western media have played in our understanding of the Soviet Union, from the Russian Revolution of October 1917 to its dissolution in 1991. It will set out two related but distinct elements in the media's Cold War, interpretive framework: the 'enemy image' of the Soviet Union and how it was used in the West to make sense of its relationship with the Soviet Union. With that established, it then presents four chapters (Chapters 3 to 6) which examine different aspects of how the media have responded to the emergence from chaos in the 1990s of a new Russia determined to reassert its power and confidence under the leadership of President Vladimir Putin. Stretching across 20 years, the book focuses mainly on the daily press in the UK, with reference also to the *New York Times*. This delivered a total sample of 3,177 newspaper items, using the Nexis database of British daily newspapers and the *New York Times* online archive.

Chapter 3 analyses coverage of all five presidential elections in Russia since Putin came to power in 2000, including that in 2008 when he stood down according to constitutional obligation but became prime minister under the new president, Dmitry Medvedev. Its focus is primarily on the way in which Putin's image was constructed from the start in very negative Cold War terms (total number of items: 485).

Chapter 4 examines the reporting of Putin's relationship with his political opposition at home and abroad. The analysis includes four case studies, looking at coverage of the assassination in Moscow of two opposition figures: the journalist, Anna Politkovskaya, in 2006; and the politician, Boris Nemtsov, in 2015; and the fate of two former Russian intelligence officers based in Britain: the murder of Alexander Litvinenko in London, 2006; and the attempted murder of Sergei Skripal in Salisbury, in 2018 (total number of items: 656).

The next two chapters turn attention to Putin's relationship with the West. The analysis in Chapter 5 focuses on the reporting of the Russian leader in conflict and how the West responded to this. It includes five case studies, looking at coverage of the opening phase of the Second Chechen War, 1999–2000; the Russo–Georgian War, 2008; Russia's annexation of the Crimean peninsula from Ukraine and the downing of Malaysia Airways Flight MH17, in 2014; and Russia's support for President Bashar Assad, in 2012 (total number of items: 1,649).

Chapter 6 includes analyses of six case studies, looking at coverage of Putin's meetings with successive US presidents from Bill Clinton in 2000 to Donald Trump in 2018. It will highlight the way in which coverage of the Russian leader's summit meetings with Donald Trump marked something of a paradigm break, with even the conservative press taking a critical position towards the US President against the background of growing tensions between Europe and the USA over national security and defence spending (total number of items: 387).

The final chapter – 'The Makings of a New Cold War?' – draws on material from the samples stated above to assess the extent to which the press in Britain have established a new Cold War framework of interpretation for understanding the relationship between the West and Russia. The focus will be on the voices in the editorial pages – editorials, columns and guest columns – and how they compete to offer an analysis and explanation of this relationship. Is it merely specific to the disposition of Vladimir Putin as the Russian leader, locking him into a Cold War position as a threat to the West; in other words, is it a transient phase of relationship that will change again after President Putin finally stands down in 2024? Or does most of this editorial content offer an alternative analysis that looks beyond conceptions of Cold War to something more akin to the imperial struggles of the nineteenth century, in other words a 'Great Powers' game? Of course, the ultimate question is this: is there any alternative to these explanations, one that switches the focus from Russia to the West and challenges its actions and policies to offer a more critical and nuanced perspective on this long-running, problematic relationship?

2

The Cold War, the Media and the Enemy Image

Having an enemy is important, not only to define our identity but also to provide us with an obstacle against which to measure our system of values and, in seeking to overcome it, to demonstrate our own worth. So when there is no enemy, we have to invent one. ... And so we are concerned here not so much with the almost natural phenomenon of identifying an enemy who is threatening us, but with the process of creating and demonizing the enemy.

(Umberto Eco, 2013: 2)

The certainty for journalism throughout the Cold War was the bipolar world of East and West, Communism and capitalism, because it provided a framework of interpretation – a way of seeing the world and of reporting international relations – that conformed to predictable patterns and narrative outcomes. Pierre Bourdieu's idea of 'master patterns' is useful here, by which he means 'an infinite number of individual patterns directly applicable to specific situations' (1972: 192). The problem, Bourdieu argues, is that while such master patterns help us to sustain thought, they may also take the place of thought. While they should help us to master reality with minimum effort, 'they may also encourage those who rely on them not to bother to refer to reality' at all (Bourdieu, 1972: 192). This is a crucial point when we come to consider the role of the Western media during the Cold War. They constructed their Cold War imagery both through *and* within one such 'master pattern' or interpretative framework. If we accept this, we have to make a distinction between the actual framework, the 'deep structures' of thought and action, and the instrumental 'enemy image', which served to rationalise it. It would be wrong to argue that they are one and the same. The Cold War was characterised by alternating periods of hostility and détente and these determined the functional utility of the enemy image. But periods of détente did not signify crisis in the fundamental ideological framework; that remained constant throughout the conflict.

THE ENEMY IMAGE AND ITS ORIGINS

As George Gerbner argues, in the context of the Cold War, the enemy image 'has deep institutional sources and broad social consequences. It projects the fears of a system by dramatising and exaggerating the dangers that seem to lurk around every corner. It works to unify its subjects and mobilises them for action' (1991: 31) and, as Edward Thompson argues, helped dehumanise the 'other side' (1982). The enemy image has been projected across a range of literary and media forms: in popular fiction, press and broadcasting, television drama and cinema. They have projected images of the superpowers in simplistic binary opposition of good and evil: Uncle Sam versus Ivan the Terrible, the Eagle versus the Bear (an image used in a Pentagon video on the arms race), the Promised Land versus the Evil Empire. In the Soviet Union, the images were reversed. The West represented the kind of economic and social inequalities that the Russian Revolution sought to overthrow. Its shortcomings were minimised with persistent reference to capitalist exploitation and Western imperialism.

The sources of the Cold War enemy image are rooted in the West's response to the October Revolution in 1917. Walter Lippmann and Charles Merz (1920) carried out a content analysis of the *New York Times*' coverage of the revolution and its aftermath, over a three-year period from March 1917 to March 1920. They found that it shifted in tone and disposition in the sample period, from naïve excitement and optimism as the newspaper tried to work out if these momentous events, two revolutions in a matter of months, would see Russia stay on the allied side in the last phase of the First World War. But the aftermath of the Bolshevik revolution and the failed Allied intervention in 1918, signalled a critical fracture in relations between

East and West. The authors found that the newspaper appeared perpetually convinced that the new regime would collapse – an assumption founded in nothing more than wishful thinking. Thus, it reported 30 times that Soviet power was on the wane; 20 times that counter-revolution was imminent; 14 times that regime collapse was underway; four times that Lenin and Trotsky were ready to flee Russia; three times that they had actually fled; three times that Lenin had been imprisoned; once that he was about to retire; and once that Lenin had been assassinated (Lippmann and Merz, 1920: 10–11). Reports of 'the Bolshevik menace' and 'the Red Peril' had mounted to such an extent that in the last year of the sample period, the *New York Times* was suggesting something approaching an invasion of the world. Lenin was apparently planning invasions of India, Poland and Persia, while also preparing for war with Britain (Lippmann and Merz, 1920: 40). Lippmann and Merz attributed this kind of reporting to organisational factors in the practice of professional journalism, the key theoretical impulse of their study. But what is interesting for the purposes of this study is the way in which the *New York Times* dramatised so much of its coverage in terms of the actions of individuals rather than international or geopolitical competition. In other words, the Russian Revolution was staged and promoted by the individual whims or the ideological obsessions of Lenin and Trotsky rather than something made possible by deeper, historical processes, for example, the upheaval of world war and the collapse of the old empires including the Tsarist empire itself.

But the reporting of the *New York Times*, as shown by Lippmann and Merz, was not exceptional. As Philip Knightley (2004) shows, most Western journalists and their newspapers appeared to ignore the causes and circumstances of the revolution and revolutionary politics and failed to report developments with any depth of analysis or insight; and many were compromised by their involvement in the subversive activities of Western intelligence agencies. They were reporting, mostly from outside Russia, that the Bolsheviks were doomed to fail and were without popular support. The Revolution's first great test was the allied intervention of 1918, known in mainstream, Western historiography as the Russian Civil War. Western reporting of the intervention was heavily censored and only reports sympathetic to its aims were allowed. Most dispatches, whether about Bolshevik thinking and strategy, or the course of the intervention, relied on sources close to Western governments or exiled Russian groups hostile to the revolution. With few exceptions, coverage relied on anti-Bolshevik hysteria based on rumours and black propaganda. Reporting fell into the same pattern of falsehood and exaggeration that emerged in coverage of the First World War and the Russian Revolution. Defeats of the Western alliance were reported as victories, while low morale and poor discipline in the allied armies were not reported at all. The Red Army on the other hand was reported to be near collapse and defeat even as it was in fact rolling back the allied intervention (Knightley, 2004: 142).

It was rare to find voices of dissent in the coverage. Arthur Ransome of the *London Daily News* eventually disowned self-interested sources, especially the British secret services, to report on a much more objective level. He wrote that: 'It is folly to deny the actual fact that the Bolsheviks do hold a majority of the politically active population' (Knightley, 2004: 133). He argued that the allied attitude to the revolution was wrong and that it only bred Bolshevik suspicions about the real intention of the allies (Knightley, 2004: 135).

The radical American reporter, John Reed, and Morgan Philips Price of the *Manchester Guardian* distinguished themselves with comprehensive and intelligent coverage. Philips Price reported events at the centre of Bolshevik power, providing insights into how the Russian Revolution was faring in face of the Western intervention. His reports were structured not around rumour and propaganda but were based on first-hand observations and interviews with the leadership. Both journalists served their readers with first-hand, immediate and non-judgemental accounts of a revolution in the making (see Philips Price, 1997; Reed, 1926).

Ever since the revolution, the most negative and virulent images prevailed over relatively short periods of crisis in US–Russian/Soviet relations. A longer, historical perspective on how each side defined the other points to a more dynamic process of political and cultural conflict and struggle on all fronts of the Cold War. While the Cold

War saw the picture at its blackest extreme, other periods of détente witnessed mixed images and shifting perceptions. The propaganda was successful in concealing a history of more 'normalised' relations between the USA and Russia as competing 'great powers', periods when they engaged in much more open economic, political and cultural exchange. Everette Dennis *et al.* (1991) work within a broad historical and comparative framework to examine changes in how the USA and Russia/Soviet Union saw each other from the nineteenth century. For example, while condemning the inequalities of American capitalism, Leninist journalism would also praise its productive forces, its technological advances and its great engineering feats (Zassoursky, 1991; Mickiewicz, 1991). Conversely, in the US media, images of stupid and violent Russians would mix with stories of Soviet–American cooperation and friendship, especially during the Second World War when the alliance with the Soviet Union was so crucial (Gerbner, 1991; Lukosiunas, 1991; Richter, 1991; Zassoursky, 1991). Such periods of Cold War thaw, or détente, brought with them a certain transformation of mutual image and perception and even significant political progress, the most notable and interesting being the ascendency in 1985 of Mikhail Gorbachev as a new type of Soviet leader, one who in the words of British Prime Minister, Margaret Thatcher, the West 'could do business with'. Gorbachev understood that the Soviet Union could no longer survive the extreme demands of its Cold War competition with the West and that it needed to radically reform its economy and society by way of what he described as *perestroika* and *glasnost*. In both personality and intent, Gorbachev projected a positive image and intent to the West, but few predicted the far-reaching consequences this was to have in just a matter of six years.

Perestroika, or 'reconstruction', referred to the idea that the problems with the Soviet economy, the gap, for example, between supply and demand, could only be solved by a radical rethink of economic policy. *Glasnost*, or 'openness', referred to a new period of liberalism in Soviet life and culture in which criticism and debate were allowed as long as they were constructive, and as long as people suggested better alternatives for making the revolution work for the betterment of all the people. *Glasnost* was the means by which the public could be mobilised into supporting the programme of reforms proposed under *perestroika* and projecting a more positive image to the world was a vital part of the task. Not least among these changes was the transformation of the Soviet leader from Evil Emperor to Nice Guy. In the image-conscious West, Mikhail Gorbachev achieved 'superstar' status. Compared to his predecessors, he was young, photogenic and charismatic. But, as he toured the capitals of the West to popular acclaim, he became a propaganda liability for the West. Take, for example, his performance vis-à-vis Ronald Reagan during the Moscow Superpower Summit in May 1988. One of the highlights of the summit in this respect was his joint walkabout with Ronald Reagan around the Red Square. Here is how BBC News and ITN compared the two men:

> *Newscaster:* 'Mr Gorbachev saw the chance to win a few hearts and grabbed it with both hands (TAKES A CHILD IN HIS ARMS). All Mr Reagan managed was a handshake. Like before, and more so here in Moscow, Mr Gorbachev is tending to out-stage Mr Reagan. He's a lot quicker with the repartee although Mr Reagan still scores the odd point' (REAGAN PUTS AN ARM ROUND GORBACHEV'S SHOULDER).
>
> (BBC, *Newsnight*, 31 May 1988)

> *Reporter:* 'For all the world it looked like the two superpower leaders were campaigning together on a joint ticket, Mr Gorbachev producing a small boy from the crowd and bearing him aloft for a handshake with the President in true American election style. Mr Reagan appeared so taken with the moment that he threw his arm around the Soviet leader's shoulders.'
>
> (ITN, 31 May 1988, 17.45)

On the last day of the Moscow Summit, Gorbachev held a long news conference, speaking to the Western media on all issues, sometimes without notes; and even stopping to reorganise the seating arrangements in order to surmount problems with the simultaneous-translation facility. The event contrasted with Ronald Reagan's poorly attended news conference at the US Embassy, where the president appeared to struggle with the issues and was criticised for selecting favoured US journalists for questions. The comparison was highlighted in some sections of the British news media. ITN described Gorbachev's performance as 'an extraordinary tour de force without a note' (1 June 1988, 13.00). The BBC observed 'a man in control: quick-witted, dynamic, formidable' (*Newsnight*, 1 June 1988, 22.30). The newspapers on 2 June also compared performances. The *Guardian* reported that 'Gorbachev was masterful and ... Reagan was genially feeble, even by his own modest standards'. The *Independent* judged Reagan's conference as 'deeply embarrassing' and 'a flop'; although a more sympathetic account in *The Times* concluded that his 'rambling answers, inconclusive sentences, hesitations, and apparent difficulty in grasping the point of many questions' were 'due to fatigue'. Gorbachev's popularity and credibility rating in Europe was rising as Reagan's was flagging: the US leadership role was under symbolic assault. This was especially significant at a time when NATO planners were arguing for 'modernisation' of the alliance's nuclear forces in Western Europe to defend against the Soviet threat.

The Soviets also showed they had learned some useful lessons in Western-style news management. When in Moscow for the superpower summit, President Reagan was scheduled to meet dissidents at the US Embassy. But the Kremlin announced a major news conference with the famous dissident, Andrei Sakharov, to take place a few days later, on 3 June 1988. At the same time, they set up an interview for the Western news media with controversial Soviet politician, Boris Yeltsin. That evening, the main news bulletins were dominated by the dramatic attack Yeltsin made on conservative members of the Politburo. It was reported as an exciting, sensational departure from the normal conduct of Soviet politics, and as a story in its own right. Yeltsin, unknown to Western publics at the time, came across as a colourful personality with an interesting story to tell. His 'struggle for the people against the system' engrossed journalists and 'experts' on the Soviet Union alike. In marked contrast,

Reagan's meeting with Soviet dissidents was only mentioned in a general round-up of the main summit events of the day and seemed rather routine set against the dramatic news of Sakharov's press conference and the sensational Yeltsin interview.

The West could legitimise its stance on nuclear weapons as long as the Cold War prevailed, but the new détente undermined the tactic considerably. The solution was to project 'evil' and 'instability' from unseen metaphysical forces to what was visible. Gorbachev was a 'nice guy' and the Soviet people no doubt wanted peace and friendship, but the West had to be careful. The empire still had a long way to go before it could be trusted on Western principles of human rights. Its unprecedented social and economic reforms brought their own instabilities, hence the oft-quoted truism that an empire is at its most dangerous when it is reforming itself from within. Once again, the Moscow Summit provides an illustration of how this rhetoric worked. It was originally arranged to mark the ratification of the Intermediate Nuclear Forces Treaty (INF Treaty), concluded in Washington the previous year to reduce and eventually eradicate their stocks of intermediate- or medium-range nuclear forces. The next logical step was further progress in talks for a long-range, strategic arms treaty (START), which, if agreed, would have profound implications for superpower relations and the entire basis of the Cold War. However, talks in Geneva had ground to a halt over America's refusal to include its sea-launched missiles in the negotiations. For the USA, talking about START was out. So what did the media report? At events like superpower summits, disputes over complex issues in arms control could be eclipsed by other distracting themes. For example, the *impasse* over START at the Moscow Summit was explained with wider reference to human rights, and to the future of Gorbachev and his reform proposals.

In advance of the summit, the US news management strategy was to tap into the powerful ideological connotations that the concept of human rights carried, and which easily filtered through to routine Cold War news. Thus, Ronald Reagan set the US agenda for the meeting when he stopped over in Helsinki to give a speech commemorating the Helsinki Accords of 1975. Although human rights protocols formed only a part of the Accords, Reagan focused on them exclusively. He accused the Soviet Union of failing to live up to them since signing. On the basis of his speech, and his plan for an unofficial meeting with Soviet dissidents in Moscow, the Western news media dubbed the occasion, The *Human Rights Summit*, in bullets on 27 May, before it had even started. 'Human rights is his theme', said the BBC headline (BBC, 13.00); 'President Reagan ... has put human rights at the top of the agenda', announced ITN (13.00). Reagan was successful in framing the human rights theme with wider issues. The BBC led with his view that 'international security cannot be separated from human rights' (18.00). In contrast, the Soviet position was reported as a negative, ritual response to the preferred US agenda, not as an equally valid contending viewpoint. Channel Four News reported that the Soviets could only 'respond predictably' with 'ritual denunciations of the speech' (Channel Four News, 19.00). Accounts of internal Soviet affairs were framed in a similar way. For example, some reports on *glasnost* and *perestroika* focused on their destabilising influence over Soviet politics and their impact on Western assumptions about Soviet society. This, in turn, undermined the certainty and predictability of East–West relations and the Cold War system. As one reporter put it, 'It was simpler for NATO when the Bear was always growling. The question now is how should the West react?' (*Newsnight*, 31 May 1988).

Ever alert to deception from any quarter, Western think-tanks and media pundits fulfilled their designated role as watchdogs for national security. Zassoursky refers to timely publications like *The Soviet Propaganda Machine* and *Mesmerized by the Bear: The Soviet Strategy of Deception* (1991: 18). Caspar Weinberger, a 'Cold Warrior' with regular access to British television news, told Channel Four News that the Soviets were simply using new tactics, public relations, for their old strategy of 'world domination' and that it was important for the West to 'keep (its) guard up' (Channel Four News, 2 June 1988); there was no suggestion here that the West might also be using public relations for its own strategic interests. On a similar note, the *New York Times* columnist, A.M. Rosenthal, urged US leaders to be cautious about Gorbachev, 'a man who is still the dictator of the most powerful totalitarian nation in the world' (Chang, 1991: 70). Statements like these were not just sabre-rattling by old Cold War warriors on the sidelines, they became the principal Western justifications for its rejection of Soviet initiatives on arms control.

However, negative enemy images are not always down to the Western media alone. In some cases, the Soviet Union was its 'own worst enemy' when it came to putting its case across to Western publics. McNair (1988) considers some of the constraints faced by Western correspondents when reporting *from* the Soviet Union during the new Cold War and, conversely, the failure or inability of the Soviet authorities to shape or influence Western news coverage of Cold War issues. This helped shape 'enemy images' of the Soviet Union as much as the West's own political and cultural prejudices. The KAL incident in 1983 is a good example of this. Soviet fighter planes shot down a Korean civilian airliner over a sensitive and restricted area of Soviet airspace, believing it to be a US spy plane. Two hundred and sixty-nine passengers and crew were killed provoking outrage in the West. According to the USA, it was proof of Soviet policy to shoot down any aircraft that strayed into Soviet airspace without first asking questions. The Soviets stuck to their spy plane theory but in the early, crucial stages of the controversy, they played to the wrong audience in the wrong way. They seemed more concerned with presenting their version to their own people rather than competing with the USA in persuading the Western public that they had a credible defence. US propaganda played unopposed to more sceptical European opinion until it finally began to collapse under the weight of its own contradictions and in face of more convincing evidence from Soviet and independent sources. By then, however, it was of academic interest; the Western media had lost interest in the story (McNair, 1988: 8off. and 95ff.).

So despite the new insights into Soviet life and culture that the policy of *glasnost* offered the West, and despite the new spirit of East–West détente, the ideological fundamentals of the Cold War system and its interpretive framework remained firmly in place for most of the Gorbachev era. What few anticipated, however, was how the relative liberalism that *glasnost* allowed in the Soviet Union had created the conditions for popular protest in the countries of Eastern Europe. In 1989, the people of Poland, East Germany, Czechoslovakia and Hungary took to the streets to demand more freedom and more democracy, building an unstoppable momentum that climaxed on 9 November with the fall of the Berlin Wall, the most abiding, visual symbol of the Cold War.

THE EAST EUROPEAN REVOLUTIONS:
END OF THE OLD COLD WAR?

The year 1989: the year of revolution in Eastern Europe. The emergence of a competitive democratic opposition was very newsworthy for countries which had been governed by the one-party state for so long. It was a compelling story for journalists, one that provoked a sense of 'history in the making' and the challenge of interpreting such fast-paced events. To offer some historical perspective to this, we might refer back to Morgan Philips Price's reporting of the Russian Revolution. In a passage from his memoirs, he offers an insight into the problem of Western reporting, including his own, when he reflects on the sense of astonishment and disbelief at what he and his colleagues were witnessing:

By 9 November, it was clear that power in Petrograd (St Petersburg) was actually in the hands of the Military Revolutionary Committee. This all seemed to me at the time very ridiculous, and I wanted to laugh at what had happened in the previous three days. I was unaccustomed to the atmosphere of revolution. I tried to imagine a committee of common soldiers and workers setting themselves up in London and declaring that they were the Government, and that no order from Whitehall was to be obeyed unless it was countersigned by them. I tried to imagine the British Cabinet entering into negotiations with the Committee for the settlement of the dispute, while Buckingham Palace was surrounded by troops and the Sovereign escaped from a side-entrance disguised as a washerwoman. And yet something of this sort in Russian surroundings had actually happened. It was almost impossible to realise that the century-old Russian Empire was actually dissolving before one's eyes with such extraordinary lack of dignity.

(Philips Price, 1997: 93)

We get the same mix of drama, breathless excitement and sometimes disbelief in news coverage of the East European revolutions but with one essential difference. Far from suggesting how ridiculous such events would be if played out in the West, the reporting was determined to celebrate the events in Poland, Czechoslovakia, Hungary and Eastern Germany as a vindication of Western democracy.

A month after the June elections in Poland, John Simpson reported triumphant Solidarity deputies taking their seats and how, 'Suddenly there was an outburst of democracy!' (BBC1, 10 July 1989, 13.00). He watched the scenes at the Spartacus Cafe in Budapest, Hungary, 'the information centre for the brand-new opposition parties (where) "'You can't afford to miss a single day's newspapers at the moment!" someone said, "It's like a new country every day!"' (BBC, 10 July 1989, 21.00) (see Simpson, 1990). When the East German government promised 'free, universal, and multiparty' elections, the news focused on the newly legalised opposition group, 'New Forum'. This 'cutting-edge of democracy' was not so much a political party as a pressure group of politically interested professionals (Channel Four News, 9 November 1989, 19.00). Their chaotic, ad hoc news conferences provided a spectacle of Western democracy, of 'normal politics' (BBC, 9 November 1989, 21.00).

The principal theme of the East European revolutions was 'people power', which echoed the fall of the Marcos regime in the Philippines earlier that year and implied that 'the people' could achieve anything if they took to the streets *en masse* and in peaceful protest. The BBC reported the opening of the Berlin Wall as a government 'giving way to the parliament of the streets'. Even the security forces were 'forced to retreat in the face of people power' (BBC1, 10 November 1989, 21.00). On BBC's *Newsnight* programme, live from West Berlin that evening, presenter Peter Snow excitedly welcomed his reporter 'who's walking into the studio with a large brick in her hand'. It was a piece of the Berlin Wall. After years of Western neurosis about what it represented, Snow laid hands on it, priest-like, and exclaimed to his studio guests, 'I don't think this Wall's going to last as long as Hadrian's Wall! It looks pretty flimsy, doesn't it?' (10 November 1989, 22.30).

The first few scenes in the drama of the Romanian Revolution at the end of that year seemed to fit the 'people power' theme with ease: the Romanian people filmed toppling Nicolae Ceauşescu, invading his palace and throwing its contents onto the streets. When they took over state television and formed a new government live on air, the images recalled the days of New Forum in East Berlin, or Civic Forum in Prague. Of all the scenes from the East European revolutions, this seemed the closest to anarchy, to real 'people power'. But when that power was extended to the summary trial and execution of the Ceauşescus, the shaky black and white video images of their dead bodies suggested something much more sinister and calculated. Looking back on the 'revolutions' and the whole sweep of events in Eastern Europe throughout the 1990s, Alex Thomson accepts that themes of 'people power' and 'freedom and democracy' were less than adequate for explaining these fast-moving events:

Romania was the great lie there. What happened in Romania? Was it the fall of Ceaucescu? Was it the collapse of Communism? Well of course it was all of those things but in fact ... what we're actually seeing wasn't a revolution, it wasn't an upsurge of the people like the Velvet Revolution in Czechoslovakia a few weeks before. It was actually more like an in-house coup. So the Romanian example is quite a good one to bring in, in the sense that the overall, rather glib, simple conclusion that yes, it's the fall of Communism, yes, it's the fall of Eastern Europe, yes, it's the fall of the Warsaw Pact, may cover you but it won't fully explain what's going on.[1]

The events in East Germany and throughout Eastern Europe in 1989 apparently marked the collapse of the Cold War. Old certainties and assumptions – economic, political or military – became null and void. The question remains, then, whether Western public discourse has met the challenge of interpreting revolutionary change (Halliday, Curry Jansen and Schneider, 1992; McLaughlin, 1993 and 1999). John Simpson, one of the few reporters to cover all the East European revolutions, thought that this placed an onus of responsibility on the reporter when trying to make sense of such events:

> (When) the Berlin Wall came down and then the revolution in Czechoslovakia and then ... in Romania ... it makes you look at it very carefully because you know that there'll be controversy about these things for the rest of your life, so therefore you want to be absolutely certain of what you think the truth is and the reality is because people will be arguing about it for a long time and asking about it. But I just knew that that was a time when you knew history was being made. [...] I'm just profoundly glad, grateful that I was able to be there.[2]

Admiral William Crowe, Cold warrior and chair of the US Joint Chiefs of Staff, summed up the loss of Cold War certainty and its implications for US national security interests: 'This is a time of very uncertain strategic transition. The future's not what it used to be.'[3] Indeed, the West's response to the end of the Cold War was hardly revolutionary or epoch-making. Many of the institutions and organisations set up to manage the conflict are still in existence – the UN, NATO and the European Union – and they have come under considerable strain in the face of continuing economic problems and an array of global crises. The news presenter, Jeremy Paxman, remarked that it took:

> something of a leap of imagination to realise that there are some people – politicians, industrialists and, above all, generals – who've been watching the scenes in Berlin with a feeling other than joy in their hearts because the events of the last few days raise enormous potential questions.
>
> (BBC2, *Newsnight*, 10 November 1989)

He might have added Western journalists to his list of suspects because it was clear that there was no persistent, ideological framework of interpretation to replace the Cold War paradigm for reporting world events. John Simpson has argued that even in the midst of uncertainty, the role of television journalism was simply to 'reflect reality':

> 1989, like 1956 and 1968, was one when the entire world changed direction and we are still living through the consequences of that: wars, upheavals, the collapse of old systems and old certainties. And until new certainties replace them, the real world will be a place of violence and conflict and our television screens will have to reflect that.[4]

Reporting Nuclear Disarmament Protests and the Peace Movement

Several research studies show how it was possible to understand the nuclear debate in the media on a number of levels: as a propaganda battle between the superpowers (Glasgow University Media Group, [GUMG], 1985; McNair, 1988; Hallin and Mancini, 1989), or between Conservatives and Labour in the 1983 and 1987 general elections in Britain (McNair, 1988). We can also look at the contribution to the debate from the peace movement and how it was reported within the broad Cold War propaganda framework (Aubrey *et al.*, 1982; GUMG, 1985; McNair, 1988). To measure the parameters of the framework, it might be useful first to offer an example of how the nuclear debate was *not* reported.

At the height of the New Cold War and the anti-Cruise missile demonstrations in the West, the *New Left Review* published *Exterminism and Cold War*. Edited by the historian Edward Thompson (1982), this international collection of essays set out a socialist critique of the nuclear arms race and addressed the problem from four points of enquiry.

1. 'the social nature and basis of [...] "exterminism" – the apparent drive of industrial civilisation towards its own self-destruction in the post-war arms race';

2. 'the respective roles and responsibilities of the two (super-powers)';

3. 'the relative importance of the distinct major theatres of the Cold War – the Far East, Europe, and the Third World'; and

4. 'the whole nexus of problems posed by the quest for a realistic way out of the looming dangers of "Exterminism and Cold War"'

(Thompson, 1982: xi)

The mainstream media, by contrast, offered the narrowest possible interpretation. They reported that the nuclear weapon was a defensive deterrent against the Soviet threat of invasion, domination or even nuclear annihilation. Andrew Wilson, defence correspondent with the *Observer*, noted the culture of fascination with nuclear weapons and weapons technology among defence correspondents in general. As with all lobby correspondents, journalists on the defence beat came into regular contact with officials in the 'defence community' and in many instances forged lasting friendships. They became immersed in a defence culture that, as Wilson argues, 'provided the essential framework within which to pursue peace-time planning for operations involving the death of millions' (in Aubrey, 1982: 37).

Coverage of the nuclear debate was underwritten by strict adherence to the rules of a crude numbers game (GUMG, 1985; McNair, 1988). The debate became so abstract and quantitative that it distracted from an underlying, qualitative concept of 'first use' or the 'pre-emptive strike'. This assumed that a limited nuclear war could be fought and won by such 'overwhelming force' that the enemy would never have a chance to retaliate. As long as the public understood that the goal of arms control was to ensure 'nuclear parity' between East and West – each side having a rough equivalence of nuclear weapons – they would not think too much about what the weapons were designed for or about the capability of a particular missile over and above its counterpart on the other side – unless of course there was an alternative source of information and argument, such as the peace movement.

The peace movement in Britain was a broad umbrella grouping of intellectuals, politicians, the Greenham Common women and the Campaign for Nuclear Disarmament, CND, most of whom were labelled as 'extremist' or 'unpatriotic'. Other religious or establishment figures were labelled either as 'naive' and 'idealistic', or as 'hysterical' and 'mad' (Sabey, 1982: 55). One television news reporter described them as 'at best misguided, at worst dangerous and subversive' (McNair, 1988: 178). Ministry of Defence propaganda linked the peace movement to the extreme left and claimed that the CND was directly funded by the Soviet Union with the aim of undermining Western security policy. Indeed, to express any kind of opposition and dissent against the 'nuclear deterrent' was to go against the interests of 'national security'. For example, in order to discredit a big disarmament protest in October 1981, sections of the media framed it as a domestic security threat in that it would tie up scarce police resources and leave Britain vulnerable to attack not from the Soviet Union but from the Irish Republican Army (IRA). As a *News of the World* columnist complained: 'at a time when the risk of IRA attack is high, why allow people like the CND to hold a massive demonstration? Yesterday's march tied up more than 1,000 policemen. No wonder the bombers keep getting away with it'. The *Sunday Telegraph* reported that, 'Thousands of police, including helicopter patrols, kept watch amid fears that the demonstration could provide cover for another IRA bomb outrage' (Sabey 1982: 60). Similar labelling was applied to the much more narrowly based, middle-class, middle-aged nuclear freeze movement in the USA (Entman and Rojecki, 1993; Gitlin, 1980).

Another significant feature of coverage at this time was the prevailing structures of access in the media. These were such that voices supporting the official view were able to dominate media coverage and define the issues from their perspective. Although alternative viewpoints did filter through, these were usually framed negatively. Whereas spokespersons for the official perspective were interviewed at length and without serious inquiry, representatives of the peace movement were subjected to close scrutiny and repeated interruptions.

Official propaganda also extended to public relations stunts by senior politicians which attracted significant media coverage (GUMG, 1985; McNair, 1988). One notable example was during

Easter 1983 when the then Secretary of Defence Michael Heseltine staged a visit to the Berlin Wall as peace marches took place all over Britain. The intent was clear: to draw a counterpoint between the West defence of freedom and the peace movement's attempt to undermine the means of maintaining that defence – the nuclear deterrent. At around the same period, Prime Minister Margaret Thatcher declared that the women holding hands around the military base in Greenham Common would be far better off holding hands around the Berlin Wall. McNair points to another tactic that the British government adopted with considerable success: that was to simply ignore the peace movement in the hope that the media would lose interest. A demonstration, in 1984, against the Trident nuclear submarine system in Barrow-in-Furness was attended by 20,000 people, yet ITN only gave it a summary item lasting a few seconds; the BBC did not report it all (McNair, 1988: 179). The Glasgow University Media Group concluded that the implicit, damning assumption underpinning news coverage of the peace movement was, 'It won't change anything' (GUMG, 1985: 234). Throughout the New Cold War of the 1980s, each side was commonly depicted peering at the other over the Berlin Wall with fear and suspicion (McNair, 1988; Dennis *et al.*, 1991). While such portrayals were prevalent throughout the Cold War, they had a universal utility that could be applied to any external threat for the containment of the domestic populace (Chomsky, 1989: 28; see also Gitlin, 1980; Parenti, 1983).

However, the collapse of the Soviet Union in 1991 opened up a decade in which a new, independent Russia struggled through economic, political and social chaos, while the West proceeded to live in a fantasy world in which it claimed ideological triumph in the Cold War or, to borrow from the title of Francis Fukuyama's celebratory book, *The End of History and the Last Man* (1992). For the first president of the newly formed Russian republic, Boris Yeltsin, there was little to celebrate amid the economic and social chaos, apart perhaps from his brief moment of glory in 1993, when he had the army bomb the White House, the Russian parliament building, in the face of an alleged coup by opposition parties, primarily the Communist Party of the old Soviet Union. Yeltsin emerged the victor in that struggle but, ultimately, he presided over economic chaos throughout his two terms in the 1990s and became subject to the seemingly all-powerful oligarchs – opportunists who took advantage of the economic chaos to build for themselves a powerbase that appeared to be unassailable and free from democratic accountability. In 1999, an infirm Boris Yeltsin appointed a new prime minister, Vladimir Putin. By the end of that year, on New Year's Eve, Yeltsin announced his early retirement due to ill health and welcomed Putin as his interim replacement until the next election, which was due to take place in March 2000. Putin went on to stand in and win that election and has gone on to become one of Russia's longest serving and powerful leaders since Stalin. But who was he?

UNDERSTANDING PUTIN'S RUSSIA

The Russian journalist, Anna Politkovskaya, opens her book, *Putin's Russia* (2004), by stating that it 'is about Vladimir Putin but not as he is normally viewed in the West. Not through rose-tinted spectacles.' Four years later, she was assassinated outside her apartment in Moscow, with many in the West seeing Putin as the chief suspect (for analysis of the media coverage, see Chapter 4). However, even a cross-section of the ever-expanding literature in the West about the Russian leader and his regime would suggest otherwise about how they are seen.

Edward Lucas (2014) charts the rise of Vladimir Putin from being a mediocre KGB officer in East Germany during the last years of the Cold War, the late 1980s, to president of Russia by the turn of the twentieth century. His popularity in the country hid the true nature of his regime (Lucas, 2014: 11) in which, amid economic recovery, 'greed was overtaking fear' with the rise of the oligarchs (Lucas, 2014: 12); and in which media and personal freedoms were being increasingly restricted (Lucas, 2014: 12–18). It was also apparent that Putin was formulating an increasingly aggressive foreign policy in which the 'New Cold War' was being fought with cash, national resources, diplomacy and propaganda (Lucas, 2014: 13). For Lucas, 'The ideological conflict of the New Cold War is between lawless Russian nationalism and low-governed, Western multilateralism' (2014: 18). According to this thesis, the West was losing the 'New Cold War' before it even noticed it had started (Lucas, 2014: 22). In the final chapter of the book, 'How to Win the New Cold War: Why the West must Believe in Itself', Lucas presents his thesis on how the West should relate to the newly resurgent Russia (2014: 269–79). First, it should recognise that one of Putin's primary aims was to divide the Western allies (Lucas, 2014: 270–1). To counter that strategy, it had to force him to recognise that there were costs involved in trading with the West. It also had to secure energy lines against Russian attempts to play-off Western dependence on its gas supplies, while its financial centres had to 'rethink how they can deal with Russian companies wanting to use them' (Lucas, 2014: 272–3). The EU and the USA also had to stop assuming that a 'deal' has always to be done with Russia, if they were to promote their own interests. Sometimes, they should simply do nothing. Taking a 'strategic pause' would be to send a powerful message to the Kremlin (Lucas, 2014: 274–7).

Interestingly, however, Lucas closes his thesis on a defiant, ideological note reminiscent of the old Cold War. For him, 'The biggest question is how to fight the war of values' (Lucas, 2014: 277):

> Yet one of the most peculiar features of the Putin years has been the number of Western commentators who are so keen to protest about the 'demonisation' of Russia and so unwilling to critique what is happening there. [...] Until we make it clear that we believe in our own values, we cannot defend ourselves against the subversion and corruption that are leaking into our citadels of economic and political power. And we stand not the slightest chance of persuading Russians themselves that the authoritarian, xenophobic and distorted version of capitalism peddled by their rulers is not a new civilisation but a dead one.
>
> (Lucas, 2014: 278–9)

On a similar note, Bill Browder warns that:

> It bears mentioning that in Russia there is no respect for the individual and his or her rights. People can be sacrificed for the needs

of the state, used as shields, trading chips, or even simple fodder. If necessary, anyone can be gotten rid of. A famous expression of Stalin's drives right to the point: 'If there is no man, there is no problem'.

(Browder, 2015: 17)

Steven Lee Myers argues that,

Without Putin, there would have been no annexation of Crimea, no war in Ukraine, no wreckage scattered about the wheat fields. This was Putin's war, and the best efforts of the Kremlin's propagandists to muddy the waters – by broadcasting false claims and conspiracy theories – did nothing to obviate the blame.

(Lee Myers, 2015: 473)

He goes on to argue that, 'For Putin, the personal had become policy.' The war in Ukraine had 'marked a fundamental break in the trajectory that he had followed', since emerging to succeed Yeltsin (Lee Myers, 2015: 475). Since then, he has been:

focused on restoring Russia to its place among the world's powers … Now he would reassert Russia's power with or without the recognition of the West, shunning its 'universal' values … as something alien to Russia, something intended not to include Russia but to subjugate it.

(Lee Myers, 2015: 475)

Shaun Walker argues that 'the particular way in which the Soviet Union disintegrated, and the vacuum of ideas and purpose it left in its wake, is undervalued when it comes to our understanding of Russia and the whole post-Soviet world' (2018: 1). With this in mind, he sets out to chart Putin's 'curation of the past in the service of the present'. This was an:

attempt to meld collective memory of the painful and complicated Soviet decades into something Russians could be proud of, particularly the elevation of victory in the Second World War to a national, founding myth. Putin had no interest in resurrecting the Soviet system, but the sense of injustice over the way it collapsed would prove a powerful rallying point.

(Walker, 2018: 9)

As Walker reminds us, paraphrasing Putin, 'only a person without a heart could fail to miss the Soviet Union, only a person with no head would want to restore it' (2018: 20).

Angus Roxburgh (2013), former Moscow correspondent for the *Sunday Times* (1980s) and the BBC (1990s), reminds readers that the negative Western view of Putin and his regime was more recent than imagined. He reminds us that at the beginning, in 2000, 'many Western leaders at first welcomed his fresh, new approach, and his willingness to cooperate and seek consensus' (Roxburgh, 2013: xiii) and attempts to chart how and why the relationship soured:

Why Putin became more and more authoritarian, how he challenged the West and how the West challenged him too; how each side failed to see each other's concerns, causing a spiral of mutual mistrust and lost opportunities. On the one hand, there is what the … West observed: Russia's political crackdown, the brutal war in Chechnya and murders of journalists, the corrupt Mafia state and growing bellicosity (Georgia and Ukraine). On the other, there is Russia's view: America's domineering role in the world, its missile defence plans, the invasion of Iraq, the expansion of NATO … And there is each side's failure of vision: Putin's inability to see any connection between his own repressions at home and the hostile reaction abroad; George W. Bush's inability to understand Russia's age-old fear of encirclement or its fury at his high-handed policy adventures.

(Roxburgh, 2013: xiii)

For the UK-based Russian academic, Dmitri Trenin (2016), part of the problem for the West has been its tendency to overrate Putin's real power. 'Most fears (in the West) about Russia are dated or groundless,' he argues, while at 'the same time, a lot of dangers linked to America's or Europe's relations with it are all too happily ignored. In other words, Russia should not be feared but, rather, always be handled with care' (Trenin, 2016: xiii). Whereas military power and global reach were key points of confrontation during the old Cold War, now these are information and geo-economics with the West way out in the lead. This, in turn, has prompted Russia to 'elect the field which it finds more comfortable – military action – and to put a premium on the swiftness and the boldness of its own steps' (Trenin, 2016: 3). Mark Galeotti (2019) also points to the West's over-estimation of Russian power. 'The prevailing tendency to see Putin as a Machiavellian grand mastermind,' he argues, 'plays to a Western fear that he is behind everything that goes wrong, and that each setback is part of some complex Russian strategy ... as a result, we run the risk of giving him too much power' (Galeotti, 2019: 13–14). Rather than follow some 'grand plan or strategy', Putin was following Facebook's Mark Zuckerberg's strategy of moving fast and breaking things, looking for 'innovative forms of disruption' to use against the West, the very act of which brings 'chaos and uncertainty' and opens up the opportunity for Putin to 'make his move' (Galeotti, 2019: 26).

From a more left-wing, sceptical perspective, Dan Kovalik looks at the 'caricature' of Putin that is being drawn for Western audiences through the media. This image of Putin, he argues, 'is being thrust before us as a symbol or proxy for a revived Russia, which we are being encouraged to hate and fear again, just as we did during the first Cold War' (Kovalik, 2017: xvii). Yet, he asks,

Where is the ideological justification for the new Cold War? There really isn't one. And that is the reason the US has had to focus so much on the personality of Vladimir Putin, imbuing him with a level of power, reach and craziness that he just doesn't have.

(Kovalik, 2017: 26)

For Peter Pomerantsev (2015), the relationship between Russia and the West is a surrender of rational thinking on both sides. 'After the

Cold War ended,' he argues, 'only one version of the future remained – some sort of default globalisation, which Russia imitated without ever believing in it, and the West went along with as long as it made money – and stopped when the financial bubble burst' (Pomerant-sev, 2015). The grim conclusion for Pomerantsev is that, now, the 'facts become unnecessary. They are, after all, unpleasant things, reminders of one's mortality and limitations. How much more fun to throw rational thinking to the wind' (Pomerantsev, 2015: ix–x).

Pomerantsev's pessimism is a postmodern response to chaos and there are times when it is difficult to refute amid the rise of divisive populism in both Russia and the West. The enemy images of Putin as a 'madman', a 'gangster' and an 'old Cold Warrior' now seem to compete in Western public discourse with equally negative percep-tions of US President Donald Trump as a master of chaos in terms of both domestic and foreign policy. While the West's political, military and security establishments worry about Russia, or about North Korea, Trump appears to dismiss them, while talking much tougher about Iran where there is an international consensus in place about managing that country's nuclear and foreign ambitions into the future. However, this new era of relative ambiguity in the West about who is the friend and who is the enemy needs to be tested against reality, time and evidence. In this book, the focus is on the media's construction of Vladimir Putin as the leader of the modern West's oldest enemies – Russia and, before that, the Soviet Union. Chapter 3, then, will present an analysis of the media portrait, in Britain and the USA, of this man as the enemy with reference to the reporting of the four presidential elections in which he stood and won: 2000, 2004, 2012 and 2018. The chapter also looks at the election of 2008 in which, obedient to constitutional law, Putin stood down and gave way to his political ally Dmitry Medvedev, a man considered in the West to be nothing more than Putin's puppet.

3

Putin is Russia – Russia is Putin: Reporting the Presidential Elections, 2000–2018

On 31 December 1999, President Boris Yeltsin resigned from office, just three months before the official end of his second and last term. In accordance with constitutional law, he was replaced on an interim basis by Vladimir Putin, a man unknown to most Russians and to the West, until the next presidential election scheduled for 26 March 2000. He went on to stand in that election, which he won with 53 per cent of the vote, and the next in 2004, which he won with 71.9 per cent. However, the Russian constitution prohibits a sitting president from seeking a third successive term so, in 2008, he made way for Dmitry Medvedev, of the United Russia party, who won by 71.2 per cent. One of his first acts as president was to appoint a new prime minister: Vladimir Putin. It was an arrangement greeted with scepticism among Western observers. In December 2008, Medvedev's administration passed through an amendment to the constitution that extended the term of the presidency from four to six years, effective from the next election due in 2012. Again, few political observers or journalists in Russia and abroad were surprised when Putin persuaded Medvedev not to stand for that election, in which he stood for himself and went on to win by 63 per cent of the vote. Neither were they surprised when he sought and won a fourth term in 2018. This meant that Putin would be in office as President of Russia until 2024, making him the longest serving and most powerful Russian leader since Stalin.

This chapter will look at Western media's construction of Putin's image, from his first election as president, in 2000, to his last victory in 2018, keeping him in power at least until 2024.

PUTIN'S IMAGE

The analysis that follows here is based on the media sample described in Chapter 1. It is structured around three principal themes: the evolving image of Vladimir Putin, from his arrival on the world stage with his first election as president in 2000 to his latest election in 2018; the democratic validity of the elections and thus the legitimacy of his terms of office; and what his power has meant to the West. Overall, it examines the extent to which the reporting plays into and interchanges with our image and understanding of both the man and his country.

On 25 March 2000, on the eve of the presidential election, the *Guardian* referred to the campaign image of Putin as a 'doting family man, dog-lover, vodka tippler, karate chopper, ladies' man, and really, one helluva of a fun guy to be around.' But as to who he really was, the paper concluded that 'we and the Russian people still do not know'. *Observer* columnist, Neal Ascherson, focused on Putin's self-professed, 'weakness for monarchy' and his rapid rise to power without trying, 'something almost unknown in the modern democratic or undemocratic world.' For Ascherson, the historical parallel with the tsars was hard to escape:

> Once there was an ascetic young tsar, who came to the throne determined to deal with the rich, corrupt boyars who threatened the survival of Russia. Like Putin, he had pure moral ideals, but a state too weak to carry them out without using tyrannical violence. His name was Ivan IV, remembered as Ivan the Terrible.
>
> (Ascherson, *Observer*, 26 March 2000).

The *Sunday Express* described him as 'the cold-eyed ruler of Russia', 'a cold, calculating ... spy who sought to undermine freedom in the West'; with 'his dark past, his sinister look', he was 'straight out of KGB central casting'. The editorial declared Putin's smile to be as 'enigmatic as that on the Mona Lisa. What lies behind it remains a mystery' (26 March 2000). The *Daily Express* ran with the same theme: 'Iron Man Putin ... comes across as stern and colourless, often cold ... the archetypal secret policeman'. In his column for the paper, Peter Hitchens called Putin 'the Kremlin leader (the West) deserves – a hollow-cheeked, taciturn, secret policeman scowling out at us from the jacket-pocket of the Russian military-industrial-security complex' (27 March 2000).

According to the *Guardian*, Vladimir Putin, 'The spy who would be king' and 'Russia's latest strong man', was a 'shrewd outsider', who contested his first election by 'unabashedly milking the appeal implicit in the image of the KGB agent as the glamorous, shadowy hero of the Soviet state (and) as Russia's answer to James Bond' (25 March 2000). He was an 'authoritarian figure' denounced by his critics as a 'war monger'; 'a KGB staffer, with clear blue eyes and authoritarian tendencies strong enough to bomb one of Russia's republics (Chechnya) back into the middle ages' (27 March 2000). The *Independent* described him as a 'Sphinx without a riddle', 'a man of mystery', whose 'cold smile and athletic stride convey a sense of energy and authority'. In an editorial after the election, the paper remarked that, 'The Western enthusiasm for Mr Putin is difficult to understand. As befits a spy, his track record is almost invisible'. The 'jury was still out,' it said, 'though the signs are not good' (28 March 2000). The *Times* was much more toned-down in its assessment of Putin the man, noting only that his victory made him 'the youngest Russian leader for 75 years, and also unique in his abhorrence of vodka and passion for regular exercise' (28 March 2000). The *New York Times* puzzled over the contradiction between the man and his apparent popularity among Russians, reporting that:

> the spare, dour 47-year-old former chief of domestic intelligence, has captivated the public and utterly confounded political sages since his vault from near-total obscurity. No one expected a man unschooled in politics and so bland in personality and appearance to seize the Russians' imagination.
>
> (*New York Times*, 27 March 2000)

The paper concluded that the answer might lie in what Putin represented to his voters: 'His calm decisiveness, apolitical manner and comparative youth contrasted favorably with the bombast, Kremlin maneuvring and indecision of the final years of an increasingly infirm Mr. Yeltsin' (*New York Times*, 27 March 2000).

Putin's first, four-year term of office was marked by struggles at home to manage the economy, repress political opposition and hold to account the 'oligarchs' – the businessmen and speculators who made vast fortunes on the back of a decade of economic chaos and a prevailing culture of corruption. This was all while overseeing a brutal war against nationalist and Islamic militia in the autonomous republic of Chechnya. When he stood for a second term as president in 2004 (14 March), he was a member of the new United Russia party, founded in December 2001 by his close political ally, Dmitry Medvedev. His re-election was widely predicted. In the media, there appeared to be two predominant views of what his victory meant: his genuine popularity in the country but also widespread unease about the kind of regime he was building.

The *Times* reported the appeal of Putin's 'dry, Soviet-style nonspeak and macho, sometimes vulgar, outbursts ... his judo black belt and KGB background ... and the arrest of the oligarch, Mikhail Khodorkovsky' (13 March 2004). When the scale of his victory became clear, the paper reported that Putin 'has steadily outmanoeuvred his rivals to become one of the most popular, and powerful, Russian leaders in living memory' (*Times*, 15 March 2004). But while his increased mandate might help 'drag Russia out of post-Soviet poverty and chaos', his authoritarian disposition raised 'the spectre of autocratic rule' ('Ghosts of the Tsars Loom over Putin's Election Landslide', *Times*, 15 March 2004). The *Sunday Telegraph* explained that he was 'riding a wave of support from women beguiled by his sobriety and his promise of a stable future'; and although he cut 'an unlikely sex symbol', he was cherished for his restraint in his personal life as much as his machismo' (14 March 2004). And for the *New York Times*, 'Putin cruised to a second term on Sunday in an election that had never been in doubt and that consolidated his centralized control of power in Russia' (15 March 2004).

In an op-ed for the *Sunday Telegraph*, the political analyst Anders Åslund argued that the 'big question is not whether Putin's system can survive – it cannot – but whether Putin's restoration of Tsarism is a brief nightmare which will be followed by a new liberalisation' ('President Putin's Imitation of a Tsar is Doomed to Failure', 14 March 2004). Patrick Cockburn of the *Independent* noted his public style: 'He walks with a purposeful military step and interrogates government ministers as if they were his junior officers. His blandest comments and most trivial meetings are treated with religious respect by Russian television.' But this 'carefully constructed public image obscures his personality'. The real Putin was still 'a mystery', a man 'whose instincts are authoritarian' ('Stealth and Secrecy Hallmark of Ex-KGB Man', *Independent*, 15 March 2004). The *Guardian* reported that the 'scale and inevitability of Vladimir Putin's victory has led analysts to warn that the Russian president is now as powerful as Stalin' (16 March 2004). Columnist, Anne Applebaum, warned in the *Times*:

> Don't be fooled – Putin's victory has nothing to do with democracy ... Nearly 15 years after the fall of the Berlin Wall, Russia remains both unique and opaque. If we want to understand what kind of a country it is becoming, we would do well to keep scratching beneath the surface.
>
> ('Beneath the Skin, It's the Same Old Russian Bear',
> *Times*, 15 March 2004)

As Putin's second term came to an end in 2008, he observed the constitutional rule prohibiting a president from standing for a third successive term. But he struck a deal with Dmitry Medvedev that in return for supporting his nomination as candidate in the forthcoming election, Medvedev would in turn appoint him as prime minister. It was an arrangement of convenience that dominated Western media reporting of the election. Constitutionally, the office of prime minister carries fewer powers than that of the president and all of those are restricted to domestic policy. The media, however, seemed in no doubt that Putin was still in charge. Both the *Guardian* (1 March 2008) and the *New York Times* (3 March 2008) described Medvedev simply as 'Putin's protégé'; but the *Guardian* reported after the election that 'Medvedev is expected to follow Putin's lead ... allowing his mentor to rule from behind the scenes. Medvedev hinted last night at the formidable power Putin would continue to wield, promising a "direct continuation" of his mentor's policies' (3 March 2008).

However, most of the media preferred the word 'puppet' to describe Medvedev and his power-relationship with Putin. Two days before the election, the *Independent* editorial felt confident to declare the winner: Dmitry Medvedev, 'the man widely known as Putin's puppet' (29 February 2008). For Tony Halpin in the *Times*, the 'more intriguing question for many is whether Mr Medvedev emerges as a forceful president in his own right or remains a puppet prince to the real power behind the throne ... Prime Minister Putin' (1 March 2008). Halpin also compared the two men in terms of their relative insecurities:

> Mr Putin's image as a cold-eyed former spy and judo black belt compensates for his relative lack of stature at 5ft 7ins. Mr Medvedev is three inches shorter and has been given lessons in how to walk and talk like his mentor to cut a more imposing figure.
>
> (*Times*, 1 March 2008)

The image training was comically yet uncomfortably apparent in Norma Percy's four-part documentary for the BBC, *Putin, Russia and the West* (January–February 2012). Michael Binyon reminded *Times'* readers that, 'President Putin insisted last September that he did not want his successor to be a puppet', but asked, 'did he mean it? And now that he is no longer President, will he allow his hand-picked successor any room for manoeuvre?' The question for Binyon was this: should Medvedev try to assert himself, would 'the back-seat driver (Putin) ... seize the wheel and even eject the driver'? (3 March 2008).

These questions about Medvedev's independence also framed the headlines on the new president's formal inauguration on 7 May 2008:

Plus ça change: Russia's New President (*Guardian*, online, 7 May)

A New Leader, and the Long Shadow Cast by Mr Putin (*Independent*, 7 May)

Power Struggle as Medvedev Takes Office (*Independent*, 7 May)

'Puppet President' Takes Power in Putin Job Swap (*Times*, 7 May)

Medvedev Becomes President but Putin Stays Centre Stage (*Daily Telegraph*, 8 May)

Always in His Mentor's Shadow (*Daily Telegraph*, 8 May)

President 'A Puppet' (*Daily Mirror*, 8 May)

Putin Sworn in as PM – and Russia's Real Ruler (*Guardian*, online, 8 May)

Medvedev Sworn In, but Putin Still Holds Power in Russia (*Independent*, 8 May)

Who Rules Russia? (*Daily Telegraph*, 9 May)

Does Putin Still run Russia? (*Guardian*, online, 10 May)

As many observers predicted, Vladimir Putin reasserted his ambition to be Russia's ultimate leader when it came to the next presidential election in 2012. His announcement, in December 2011, of his intention to stand provoked a public backlash, especially among the urban middle classes who took to the streets in protests right up until the election on 4 March 2012. As the day approached, the *Guardian* presented it as one in which the people away from the towns and cities, 'out there in the dominant wastes of winter ... (wanted) a chastised, humbled Putin', but were confronted with an unenviable choice: 'If not Putin, who?' (2 March 2012). Putin won the election with 63.6 per cent of the vote and gave an emotional victory speech in which he railed against the protests. He later denied reports in some sections of the domestic and foreign media that he had even shed a tear or two:

Putin Wept (*New York Times*, 4 March)

When It was all Too Much for Vladimir Putin (*Independent*, 5 March)

Why So Sad, Vlad? (*Guardian*, 6 March)

The *Daily Telegraph* went further to report that, actually, 'Putin had tears rolling down his cheeks' ('Emotional Putin Sheds a Tear', 5 March 2012). After the event, the president insisted that it was actually moisture in the eyes caused by the cold wind. In any case, the weight of coverage of the election presented a conflicted image of the man, often by the same newspaper or broadcaster. On the one hand, Putin was consolidating his power after four years in the constitutionally lesser office of prime minister. For example, the *Independent* reported Putin's victory speech under the headline: 'President, then Prime Minister, and now President Again as Russia's Most Powerful Post-Soviet Leader Reasserts his Grip' (5 March 2012). Luke Harding, in the *Guardian*, described it as 'Vladimir Putin's Brezhnev moment', from which he could 'go on and on' (5 March 2012). Alluding to the 'bad old days' of the Cold War and Soviet gerontocracy, he reminded readers that, '(Leonid) Brezhnev did 18 years, Stalin 31. Despite the whispers of revolution lapping at the Kremlin's walls, who would bet against Vladimir matching Leonid?' This, he predicted, would come down to Putin's gut political instincts:

> Confronted with the spectre of (revolution) … Putin has two options. He can try to assuage the demonstrators with the vague promise of liberal reforms, or he can use the same lugubriously repressive KGB tactics that have served on previous occasions: black PR against key opposition figures; arrests; and the perennial libel that his enemies are traitorous western stooges and US-backed 'fifth columnists'. Putin appears inclined towards the second, more thuggish, option.
>
> (Harding, *Guardian*, 5 March 2012)

On the other hand, we were told that his power was waning and that, politically, he would not survive a full, six-year term of office. One of Putin's most implacable opponents, former chess grandmaster, Garry Kasparov, told the *Times* that Putin was 'a thug … a lifelong KGB man who trusts only in the power of fear and violence … a global menace.' He concluded: 'If the so-called Western values of freedom and human rights still matter, mark tomorrow's vote as the beginning of the end of Putin's rule, not a fresh start' (*Times*, 3 March 2012). On election day, the *Sunday Times* predicted that 'bar earthquakes, famine or a plague of frogs', Putin would win but that opposition among the Russian middle class would sooner or later see him out as 'the last of the Russian dinosaurs' (4 March 2012). Another item by Mark Franchetti, the *Times'* reporter in Moscow, was headed, 'Putin Commands on Borrowed Time ... the Russian leader's power is ebbing as people tire of corruption' (4 March 2012). In the *Sun* online, the former Foreign Secretary, David Miliband, laid down a bet: 'I will wager one prediction. Whether or not Vladimir Putin wins today, he will not be celebrating a fourth term in office six years from now' (4 March 2012). And writing in the *Daily Telegraph* after the election, Edward Lucas declared that:

> Vladimir Putin has won the battle ... But he has lost the war. He cannot satisfy his own supporters. Nor can he win back those swelling the ranks of the opposition, who yearn for the justice, truth and dignity that his regime cannot provide.
>
> (Lucas, *Daily Telegraph*, 5 March 2012)

With a focus on issues such as the widespread culture of corruption in Russia and the economic problems caused by falling oil revenues, Lucas concluded that, 'The big danger for Mr Putin is that his ex-KGB cronies will see him as a liability more than an asset. His presidential term lasts six years in theory. I give him two' (5 March 2012).

The tendency to apply the assumptions of liberal democracy to a country with little or no tradition of such has been a common feature in Western media reporting before Putin, indeed throughout the Cold War. Putin saw out the full term of office in the same style, domestically and internationally, because he had a strong mandate and a knack for tuning in to the conformist instincts of a people tired of decades of instability and corruption; and tired also of Russia's image of weakness on the world stage. His annexation of Crimea in 2014 was well received in the country and the hostile reaction to it in the West seemed to make it all the sweeter. Indeed, the Western condemnations of the attempted poisonings of ex-Russian intelligence officer, Sergei Skripal and his daughter Yulia, in Salisbury on 4 March 2018, were regarded in Russia with a good degree of popular scepticism or indifference. This was just as well for Putin because the presidential election was scheduled to take place exactly two weeks later, on 18 March 2018. The question now was how the poisonings, evocative as they were of the Cold War of the 1980s, would colour the ever-evolving Western media image of the Russian leader, as he looked certain to win the election and stay in power for yet another six years. Running, this time, as an independent candidate in a bid to access a voting base beyond that of the United Russia party, on the eve of election, opinion polling showed him far in front of his nearest rivals. The result was indeed a triumph; he won 76.6 per cent of the vote, with his nearest rival, Communist Party candidate, Pavel Grudinin, winning just 11.7 per cent. It defied the previous Western predictions in 2012 that he would not even make it halfway through that term of office. In this context, one would expect universally hostile coverage in both tone and content. But there was a major difference of emphasis among British newspapers in how they framed the election. The elite newspapers on the left as well as on the right of the political spectrum focused mainly on the implications of the result for how Putin would go on to govern Russia and lead the country's relationship with the West. Also, there was a shift in tone from their coverage of previous elections going right back to Putin's first term, 2000–2004. The hostility that set the tone then was replaced by something much more measured and it lacked the negative caricatures of the Russian president so familiar up until this point.

For the *Guardian* (online), Putin had defied Western expectations and was now 'stronger than ever' (18 March 2018). An *Observer* headline stated that 'For many growing up in Russia today, Putin is the only leader they have known. They aren't about to turn against him now.' In its editorial, in the same issue, headed 'The World Must Face Up to What Putin's Victory Means', the *Observer* admitted:

the uncomfortable truth ... that Mr Putin does enjoy popular support, though exaggerated by him. Some Russians, convinced by his crude nationalism, are genuinely devoted to the new strong man for Mother Russia, while many others are frightened about what he is doing to their nation.

(*Observer*, 18 March 2018)

Janet Daley in the *Sunday Telegraph* (18 March 2018) measured Putin against US President Donald Trump. 'The US president,' she wrote, 'has been gratuitously offensive and anarchically self-contradictory (but) nothing he has done, or threatened to do, is remotely comparable with the reckless aggression of Putin's Russia.' But she also noted that both men shared a narcissistic streak, in that the more negative the world's opinion of them, the more vindicated they felt in their sense of mission. Her closing sentence: 'America First faces Russia Re-born: dangerous times indeed' (*Sunday Telegraph*, 18 March 2018). 'By means both fair and foul,' reported the *Independent*, Putin 'had eased a resounding election victory.'

The popular press, which used to be called 'the tabloids', preferred to cover Putin's election win with a view to the Skripal poisonings (see Chapter 4) and Britain's official response to them, that is, the drive for economic sanctions, diplomatic expulsions and a possible boycott of the forthcoming World Cup 2018 tournament, due to be held in Russia in June that year. Accordingly, their negative imagery and Cold War allusions persisted from their coverage of the previous elections. On the day of the election, the *Sunday Express* led on its front page with political calls for action against Russia: 'May Stands Up to Putin. PM Vows: We will never tolerate attacks on our soil by Russia. 23 UK diplomats expelled from Moscow; 1,000 oligarchs will face travel ban. PM vows to act after "'appalling breach of international law"' (18 March 2018). In an opinion piece for the *Sunday Express* headed, 'Fight Putin's Toxic Tyranny', John Woodcock MP argued that the Skripal poisonings 'showed the murderous side of Vladimir Putin's regime that is making him an international pariah.' The closing down of the British Council in Moscow, he claimed, exposed Putin's 'paranoid intolerance and obsessive hatred of anything emanating from open, law-respecting democracies'. The paper also reported worrying news for Putin that Dame Judy Dench 'gives Russian film festival the cold shoulder'. The festival normally ran in Sochi, in southern Russia, but was staged that year in London as an attempt by the organisers to improve Anglo-Russian relations. The organisers denied that it was a snub on Dench's part. The paper's rivals also led with the boycott/sanctions story in this period:

Your Move, PM. May Vows New Sanctions in Showdown with Russia (*Sun on Sunday*, 18 March)
So Vlad, We've Got May to Defend Us. Warm Heart, Acid Tongue (*Sun on Sunday*, 18 March)
Put the Boot in Putin, Theresa (*Star on Sunday*, 18 March)
PM's War on Putin 'McMafia' Millions (*Mail on Sunday*, 18 March)
Breaking Vlad (*Sun*, 19 March)
Vlad, Bad and Deadly to Cross (*Sun*, 20 March)
You're a Vlad Joke (*Mirror*, 20 March)
Put Boot in with Footie Boycott (*Mirror*, 20 March)

The *Daily Star* and the *Daily Mirror* led also with a focus on the push for an England boycott of the World Cup 2018, due to be held in Russia that June. The *Daily Star's* editorial on the issue was headed 'Give Vlad Red Card', yet on the following day (20 March 2018), it reported on the negative reaction of England fans to the call for a boycott. Most of them opposed the line the paper took and refused to be put off. In typical populist style, the paper gave voice to their opinions under the headline, 'Putin's Spies, Yobs & Safety Fears Won't Stop Our Lionheart Fans'.

The media picture of Putin that emerges from the coverage of these elections is of the 'ex-KGB man' turned 'Ivan the Terrible', determined to rule Russia with an 'iron grip' over every arm of the state and to exploit the culture of corruption by, on the one hand, facing down the powerful oligarchs while, on the other, syphoning off billions of dollars for himself. It is a picture that was becoming increasingly reflected in political debate in Britain about how to respond to the Skripal poisonings. On the day of the 2018 election, the chair of the British House of Commons' Select Committee on Foreign Affairs, Tom Tugendhat, argued in the *Mail on Sunday* that nobody should be under any illusion about the threat Putin and Russia posed to Britain:

> Russia is a rogue regime, ruled by a demagogue who thinks nothing of murdering opponents at home or abroad. Putin is leading a hostile regime and those who enable it – whether in politics, the City or elsewhere – are siding with those who threaten the British people and all those who value freedom.
>
> ('No Hiding Place for Putin's Thieves and Fraudsters',
> *Mail on Sunday*, 18 March 2018)

The second dominant theme in the coverage of these elections was the validity of the vote, with accusations from international election observers and Putin's opponents of intimidation of political opposition, systematic and widespread electoral fraud, and absolute control of the broadcast media. Such concerns were barely mentioned in the reporting of Putin's first election in 2000, when he was hardly known; but from 2004 onwards, they played a major part in framing the overall media picture in the West of the Russian president.

DEMOCRATIC LEGITIMACY

In its report on the conduct and transparency of the presidential election of 2000, the Organization for Security and Co-Operation in Europe (OSCE) noted relatively minor concerns about an apparent 'erosion of political pluralism', irregularities in the registration of candidates and restrictions on media freedom. But it concluded in its executive summary that:

> In general, and in spite of episodic events that sometimes tested the system's capacity to uphold principles of fairness and a level playing field, the presidential election was conducted under a constitutional and legislative framework that is consistent with internationally recognized democratic standards ... This election also demonstrated Russia's continuing commitment to strengthen its democratic electoral institutions, which appear to have the public's confidence and acceptance as demonstrated by the 69% turnout.[1]

The election of 2004, however, presented a very different picture. The OSCE reported that:

> While on a technical level the election was organized with professionalism, particularly on the part of the Central Election Commission (CEC), the process overall did not adequately reflect principles necessary for a healthy democratic election. The election process failed to meet important commitments concerning treatment of candidates by the State-controlled media on a non-discriminatory basis, equal opportunities for all candidates and secrecy of the ballot. Essential elements of the OSCE commitments for democratic elections, such as a vibrant political discourse and meaningful pluralism, were lacking.[2]

The Western media picked up strongly on these problems but what is interesting here is that, unlike the OSCE and other international observers, the media linked them directly to just one candidate: Putin. The *Sunday Telegraph* reported that he bribed the electorate because of his fear that voter apathy and predictions of a low turn-out at the polls would jeopardise his chances of election, 'a problem that Kremlin fixers have tackled with a promise of free groceries and pop concert tickets at polling stations' (14 March 2004). Similarly, the *Guardian* reported the result 'in an election marred by allegations of fraud, media bias, and attempts to bribe or coerce the electorate into voting' but describe the bribe as 'cheap groceries' rather than free (15 March 2004). The *Daily Mail* reported 'free holidays and haircuts' (15 March 2004). After the vote, some of the papers referred to preliminary findings of the OSCE and others that there was an overwhelming media bias in favour of Putin and widespread electoral irregularities:

Putin Sweeps to Victory in Sham Election (*Independent*, 15 March)
Election Observers Condemn Putin Victory (*Independent*, 16 March)
Monitors Report Ballot Stuffing (*Guardian*, 16 March)

Criticism of Poll Overshadows President's Election Victory (*Daily Telegraph*, 16 March)

Putin's Election Victory Helped by Biased Media (*Times*, 16 March)

Patrick Cockburn argued in the *Independent* that: 'the real significance of the Russian presidential election ... is that it is no longer an exercise in which the people genuinely chose a new leader. The democratic element ... is purely decorative' (13 March 2004). Given that Putin was obliged to stand down in the 2008 election, the link between him and the corruption of Russian democracy would be put to the test. The candidacy of Dmitry Medvedev seemed to promise a new era of liberalisation for Russia, a more plural and properly regulated democratic culture and an opening up to the West. It did not bode well, then, when in 7 February 2008, the OSCE cancelled its plans to monitor the election due to be held on 2 March. It was a protest against what it called 'unacceptable restrictions' imposed by Russia on its monitoring exercise.[3] However, the Parliamentary Assembly of the Council of Europe (PACE), sent an ad hoc delegation of election observers and published a report three weeks later that pointed to familiar issues with candidate registration, fair access among candidates to broadcast media, the secrecy of the vote and high levels of intimidating security apparatus at polling stations. But the report concluded that, overall:

> [The] voting was well administered (but for) an election to be good, it takes a good process, not just a good election day. Nonetheless, the delegation felt that, even if those concerns had been addressed, the outcome of the vote – amounting, in effect, to a vote of confidence in the incumbent President – would most probably have been the same.[4]

On the eve of the election, the *Guardian* reported serious flaws in the voting process under the headline: 'Kremlin Accused of Fixing Presidential Poll: State Workers Ordered to Vote for Putin's Protege: Ballot boxes "to be stuffed" after polls close tomorrow' (1 March

2008). The day after the election, it quoted the head of the PACE delegation, Andreas Gross, the only newspaper to mention the delegation's presence. Gross was less diplomatic than his official report was to be when he told the paper that while the election may have reflected the will of the Russian people, 'It is still not free and still not fair' (3 March 2008). The other newspapers in this sample mentioned the OSCE boycott but made no mention of PACE. In fact, the *Times* reported that:

> Fewer than 300 international observers were in Russia to monitor 96,000 polling stations across 11 times zones. Most were from former Soviet republics in the Commonwealth of Independent States, which has a history of rubber stamping the outcome of elections regardless of any violations.
>
> ('More Than 60 Million Votes for a New President – but was This Democracy?', *Times*, 3 March 2008)

In its editorial on the election campaign, headed, 'A Farcical Contest, and the Need for a United Stand', the *Independent* (29 February 2008) noted with scepticism Medvedev's high opinion poll ratings of between 70 and 80 per cent. That and the emphatic endorsement of the outgoing president, Putin, led the paper to decide that: 'In Russia you do not need an election to know the name of the next president.' It argued that the restrictions imposed on the OSCE were 'of a piece with the shackling of opposition candidates, political dissidents, human rights activists and journalists who do not work for a national media under the thumb of the Kremlin.' And it concluded:

> Things will only change if Europe adopts a more united front in its dealings with Russia. If that happens then issues such as democracy, human rights, respect for the rule of law at home and abroad, and greater respect for the sovereignty of neighbouring states, will become concerns that Russia's new president, and the man pulling his strings, will be unable to ignore.
>
> (*Independent*, 29 February 2008)

The *Times* (4 March 2008) reported that most European leaders were 'circumspect' in their reaction to the election result, but it quoted the words of French Foreign Minister, Bernard Kouchner, that 'The election was conducted Russian-style, with a victory known in advance. Medvedev,' he added, was elected with 'very surprising figures, not quite worthy of Stalin, but not bad.'

The OSCE returned to Russia to monitor the 2012[5] and 2018[6] presidential elections, reporting familiar issues in both – lack of competition, candidate registration, significant bias among the broadcast media in favour of Putin (who did little or no personal campaigning) and incidences of voting irregularities at the polls such as 'ballot stuffing'; but it also reported continuing improvements from previous elections. The Western media, however, preferred to focus on the negatives. A sample of headlines from both elections provides a snapshot of how this news angle played out to undermine Putin's legitimacy as a democratically elected president.

In 2012:

Russia's Presidential Election: Rigging is a Delicate Art (*Guardian*, 2 March)

Critics Cry Fraud as Poll Gives Putin Third Term in Kremlin (*Independent*, 5 March)

Claims of Poll Fraud Taint Putin's Victory (*Daily Telegraph*, 5 March)

Putin Poll Fault; 60% Vote Win is 'Dishonest' (*Daily Mirror*, 5 March)

Fury Grows as Observers Conclude Vote for Putin was 'Clearly Skewed': Opposition Leaders say Poll was Illegitimate Widespread Reports of Ballot-Stuffing (*Guardian*, 6 March)

'Putin is a Thief!', Cry Muscovites after Poll Landslide (*Independent*, 6 March)

And in 2018:

The region of Omsk offered free iPhones for voters who turned up in the best costumes, prompting a parade of voters who came as Santa Claus or a Roman legionnaire. One family was a hockey team.

(*New York Times*, 18 March)

Putin retains presidency as claims of 'violations' tarnish election walkover. Polls give Russian leader more than 70pc of vote and a fourth term, enabling him to rival Joseph Stalin.

(*Daily Telegraph*, 19 March)

Claims of ballot-stuffing taint Putin's coronation

(*Times*, 19 March)

Western reaction muted as allegations of vote rigging and intimidation surround controversial victory.

(*Times*, 20 March)

Rigging Claims as Putin Heads for Landslide Win

(*Daily Mail*, 19 March)

Putin Landslide Victory Tainted. Poll Violations Says Brussels

(*Daily Mail*, 20 March)

Vote Rig Fury After CCTV of Ballot Stuffing

(*Sun*, 19 March)

Vlad's Ballot Rigging Victory

(*Daily Star*, 19 March)

A THREAT TO THE WEST

The third theme to emerge from the coverage of these elections is the assessment of Putin and Russia as a military threat to the West. This was rather undeveloped in the coverage of the first election. The *Guardian* summed up the mood of uncertainty and caution. Two days after the 2000 election, it published an article headlined: 'Putin keeps west in dark on foreign policy. Air of uncertainty as world leaders queue up to make friends with the new president-elect of Russia.' It reported that Washington was 'unsure what the new leader ... stands for in the fields of economic reform, disarmament, and relations with NATO.' But it also pointed out that:

> All western leaders who have visited Moscow in the past two months have described Mr Putin as an internationalist and westerniser who wants to strengthen ties with the west after a year of estrangement caused by the Kosovo crisis, NATO expansion into eastern Europe, and Mr Putin's campaign in Chechnya.
>
> (*Guardian*, 28 March 2000)

The *Times* reported similar notes of cautious optimism in the West. A feature article assessing the likely nature of Putin's rule said that:

> Mr Putin's willingness to co-operate with foreign governments and NATO should be encouraged by the West ... America offered Mr Putin a more cautious welcome to the world stage, calling him 'a pragmatic man who should be judged on his actions'.
>
> (*Times*, 28 March 2000)

Under the heading, 'West Hopes for a Softening on Arms and Chechnya', the *Times* predicted that the new president would prioritise relations with the USA, starting with a push for a state visit by US president Bill Clinton in May that year. Most crucially, Putin might move for final victory in the war in Chechnya and push for parliamentary ratification of the Start-2 treaty on strategic nuclear disarmament and new arms talks in the near future. These might even include a shift on the 1972 Anti-Ballistic Missile Treaty, which previous Soviet and Russian administrations had refused to see altered. But there was a condition to all this. The article concluded that 'Mr Putin's success in foreign policy – particularly in coaxing a new wave of Western investment – will depend on the success of his reforms at home' (*Times*, 28 March 2000).

There were a few exceptions to the general mood of cautious positivity. The *Daily Express* reported how '[Putin] has sent shudders through the West by announcing he will pack the Kremlin with former KGB spies' (27 March 2000). Ann Leslie's column for the paper on the next day was headlined: 'Vlad The Sinister ... Russia's new leader is an ex-spy who reveres Stalin and made his name in a brutal war. We in the West should be on our guard'. Her conclusion conjured up a classic Cold War image from the not-so-distant past: 'As Russians put it, the most dangerous animal in the forest is a wounded bear. If Russia's new President fails to rescue the "wounded bear" of his motherland, it's not just Putin who should worry, but all of us' (29 March 2000).

Amid this speculation about how Russia and the West might get on, some sections of the British media reported on a development that seemed rather minor in the moment but which, by 2009, would come to prominence as a critical point of difference and difficulty between Russia and the West: the Strategic Defense Initiative, otherwise known as Son of 'Star Wars'. This was the proposal by the USA to develop a highly sophisticated defence system, using space-launched missiles to intercept and destroy land-based, offensive missiles. It had serious implications for Russia's defence because, by its very nature, it gave the USA and the West the power to effectively neutralise its entire nuclear arsenal. It also had the potential to divide the Western alliance, with the USA and the UK facing opposition to the system from France and Germany. The *Independent* reported that the USA was 'unsure what response to expect from Vladimir Putin, the new Russian President' ('Ministers Set to Back UK Role in "Son of Star Wars"', 30 March 2000).

The coverage of Putin's election for a second term in 2004 was almost free of Cold War imagery. The *Guardian* reported that, 'Echoes of the Soviet era have begun resounding in the more extreme reaches of foreign policy. The Russian bear, faced on many fronts with a hostile west, has bristled, reverting to cold war-esque confrontation' (16 March 2004); while a review of books about Putin in the *Times* was headed, 'Back in the USSR' (13 March 2004). But something happened in 2008, with the inauguration of Dmitry Medvedev on 7 May, that evoked old images of the Soviet enemy. The occasion coincided with the annual Victory Day parade, 9 May, marking the Soviet victory over Germany in the Second World War, one that claimed over 20 million Russian lives. Up until the end of the Cold War and the dissolution of the Soviet Union in 1991, the parade was on a large scale with an emphasis on displaying Soviet military power. In the post-Cold War era, it was scaled down and demilitarised, so it was a surprise to Western observers to see the new Medvedev era marked by the return to military symbolism. The Western media responded accordingly, on the next day with:

> Putin sends a shiver down the West's spine (*Daily Telegraph*)
> Russia puts on a Soviet show of might (*Daily Telegraph*)
> Just like the old days: military are back on the march for Red Square parade (*Times*)
> Tanks return to Red Square as Russia flaunts military might (*Independent*)

The *Daily Mail* described the parade as 'a chilling sight from a different age. Nuclear missile launchers and scores of tanks rolled across Red Square yesterday for the first time since the end of the Cold War' ('Kremlin's Blast from the Past; Awesome Display of Military Power in Red Square for Russia's New Leader', 9 May 2008). In an item headed, 'Back in the USSR: Big Guns Roll Through Red Square Once More', the *Guardian* reported how, 'Vladimir Putin has ... revived many potent symbols of Soviet greatness – the Soviet anthem, the red star, and – today – the 22-metre long inter-continental ballistic missile, wheeled past the GUM shopping arcade and the boutiques of Gucci and Prada' (10 May 2008). And that, 'For the first time since 1990 ... Russia's military brought out some of its kit: jeeps, tanks, long-range anti-aircraft missile systems, (recently flogged to Iran), and the Topol-M – a vast nuclear weapon capable of hitting Washington.' The article concluded that, 'Putin's apparent aim is to send a signal to the rest of the world: that after a period of weakness in the 1990s, Russia is again a great power that can't be juggled with. In short, Russia is back' (*Guardian*, 10 May 2008). The *Daily Telegraph* (7 May 2008) evoked another ghost from the Cold War past to interpret the developments of the present. In an interview with the last president of the Soviet Union, Mikhail Gorbachev, the paper reported his accusation that the United States was 'mounting an imperialist conspiracy against Russia that could push the world into a new Cold War.' This was a statement, said the *Daily Telegraph*, that 'mirrors the most belligerently anti-Western speeches of Vladimir Putin – who is said to consult Mr Gorbachev on foreign policy matters' ('Gorbachev: US at Risk of Starting New Cold War', 7 May 2008).

Dmitry Medvedev's term of office was marked by the Russian invasion of the former Soviet republic of Georgia, just months after his election, and the tense stand-off between Russia and the West that it provoked (for media analysis, see Chapter 5). But when it came to the next presidential election in 2012 and the re-election of Vladimir Putin, the Western attitude seemed to have returned to its factory setting. As we have seen in the first section of this chapter, the focus was on Putin the man, not on his foreign policy. He was a man who we were mystified and frightened by. He was the president of the largest country in the world, a leader who was built up into a tyrant; he was a despot, a new emperor, yet one losing a grip on the impossible – trying to hold together a vast empire. According to Luke Harding of the *Guardian* (2 March 2012), Putin was also the leader of a 'country dubbed by US diplomats a "virtual mafia state"'. In its editorial on another six years of Putin, the *Independent* (3 March 2012) declared that: 'The political context in which this election is being held is less stable, and the longer-term outcome less predictable than at any recent Russian election, perhaps even since the fall of Soviet communism.'

CONCLUDING REMARKS

The focus of Western media coverage at this point was not on an imminent military threat from Russia, but on the uncertainty and instability of the country and how that might play out in the long run. What is remarkable about the coverage of the 2018 presidential election, with Putin winning for yet another six years until 2024, was the almost total absence of reference or allusion to a Cold War between Russia and the West. The original assumption of this book was, of course, that having built Putin into an ideological monster, a 'folk devil', since his first steps onto the international stage in 2000, the media would still define him in 2018 as the West's public enemy No.1. This reflected a prevailing Western objection to Putin at this point of history: that he was a strong, decisive leader of the biggest country in the world and there was very little the West could do about it. So why the relative silence over the intervention in Syria? We might find a clue to the mystery, if we consider the West's fundamental misconceptions of Putin and the country he leads. Mary Dejevsky, columnist and a chief editorial writer for the *Independent*, has long experience of reporting on Russia, going back to reporting from Moscow for the *Times* during the last years of the Cold War of the 1980s. She makes a distinction between non-deliberate and deliberate misconceptions:

The non-deliberate misconception is that (Putin) somehow imposed himself on Russia and that he's not by any manner or means democratically elected. [...] Nonetheless, Putin had huge amounts of support even before the annexation of Crimea. And to my mind, Putin is the legitimate President of Russia because he's managed somehow to sense, like any good politician, where the centre of Russian opinion is at any particular point and he adjusts accordingly. So I think for all sorts of reasons he's legitimate, so to denounce him as illegitimate – a dictator, an autocrat, or whatever – that that's actually wrong.[7]

The deliberate misconception is to overestimate his real power in the country. As Dejevsky explains:

[While] Putin is strong personally – his power is very strong in the Kremlin – [but] in the country at large he's actually a weak leader because it's very difficult for anybody in the Kremlin to have all the levers of power at his disposal. This great idea that Putin can sit in the Kremlin and snap his fingers and ... people all turn around and do exactly as he says – that is completely wrong.

Russian power is extraordinarily fragmented – there are a lot of regional interests, a huge amount of corruption. One of Putin's biggest problems ever since he became leader and it's only a little less now, I would say, is that his writ doesn't rule across Russia.[8]

The following two chapters examine how the enemy image of Putin, and the misconceptions about him that Dejevsky identifies above, play into Western responses to Putin's supposed involvement in political murder at home and abroad (Chapter 4) and to Russian military interventions in Chechnya, Georgia, Syria and Ukraine/Crimea (Chapter 5).

4

Reporting Putin's Russia:
Political Opposition and Espionage

People sometimes pay with their lives for saying out loud what they think
                                        – Anna Politkovskaya, 1958–2006

Vladimir Putin's rise to power in the late 1990s has marked for the West a continuation of the Soviet model of the authoritarian state: centrally controlled from the top down in all areas of economic, political and social policy, and with an intolerance of dissent, deviance and disloyalty on the part of its citizens. This chapter analyses Western media responses to the fate of four figures, who seemed to represent an affront to the Russian state by highlighting everything the West loathed about Putin and his regime. The journalist, Anna Politkovskaya, and the pro-Western opposition leader, Boris Nemtsov, were staunch critics of Putin until they were murdered in Moscow in mysterious circumstances: Politkovskaya, in 2006, and Nemtsov, in 2015. Alexander Litvinenko and Sergei Skripal were Russian intelligence officers, who turned against the state. In very different circumstances, they ended up in England and became targets for assassination. Litvinenko was killed in London, in 2006, just weeks after the murder of Politkovskaya. The cause of death was his ingestion of a lethal dose of a rare radioactive isotope, polonium-210. Sergei Skripal and his daughter, Yulia, on a visit from Russia, survived an attempt on his life in his new home, the city of Salisbury, in 2018, having absorbed a nerve agent that experts believed was manufactured in Russia and part of a group of nerve agents called Novichok.

Common to Western media coverage of these cases was a narrative structure that mixed elements of the Cold War thriller and the crime novel or television police procedural series: a focus on the victims and the threat they may have presented to their assailant; a search for clues to solve the mystery; the identification of a prime suspect; and a determination, or lack thereof, to see the suspect brought to justice with tough action. The analyses that follow, then, are organised into two pairs: Politkovskaya and Nemtsov, representing domestic opposition to the Putin regime; and former intelligence officers, Litvinenko and Skripal, targeted in their place of asylum in the West.

OPPOSITION: POLITKOVSKAYA AND NEMTSOV

On the night of 7 October 2006, the journalist Anna Politkovskaya was murdered outside her home in Moscow by a lone gunman. It was a shock but not a surprise to journalists and others who knew and admired her work as a reporter for the Russian newspaper, *Novaya Gazeta*. Her reporting on the two Chechen Wars – 1994–1996 and 1999 until the time of her death – brought her international attention. It focused on the impact of those conflicts on innocent civilians and recalled the work of the great war correspondent, Martha Gellhorn (1908–1998).[1] Politkovskaya also focused on the economic chaos and social injustices of post-Soviet Russia but she marked herself out in particular for her unflinching opposition to the character and policies of Vladimir Putin, fuelling inevitable suspicions but little evidence that he gave the tacit but plausibly deniable order to have her killed. By the time of her murder, she had published her best work in a series of books, including the most celebrated, *A Dirty War* (2001) on the Chechen Wars, and *Putin's Russia* (2004). A posthumous collection of her later work, *Anna Politkovskaya: A Russian Diary*, was published in 2007 with a Foreword by Jon Snow, presenter of Channel Four News in the UK. He said of her: 'For many of us who continue to aspire to the highest standards of journalism, Anna Politkovskaya will remain a beacon burning bright, a yardstick by which integrity, courage and commitment will be measured' (Politkovskaya, 2007: ix)

Opposition politician and activist, Boris Nemtsov, was shot dead, late on 27 February 2015 as he crossed the Bolshoy Moskvoretsky Bridge, near the Kremlin, Moscow. He was accompanied by his partner, Anna Duritskaya, who survived unhurt. The murder happened just days before he was to lead a protest rally against Russia's corrupt economic system and its involvement in the war in Ukraine. He had built his career in the 1990s under President Boris Yeltsin, including two, one-year terms as vice-prime minister, and went on to work with activist, Alexei Navalny, in a Western-facing liberal movement that became increasingly vocal in its criticism of successive Putin administrations and their domestic and foreign policies. Immediately after Nemtsov's assassination, it was hardly surprising that his supporters pointed the finger of suspicion if not at Vladimir Putin directly then at military intelligence, an accusation that Putin bluntly dismissed.

These two assassinations seemed to symbolise the risks and dangers of opposing and criticising authority in Russia amid the chaos and economic instability of the post-Soviet era, which successive Putin administrations tried to manage and contain through a combination of authoritarian rule and appeals to Russian nationalism. Although they happened nine years apart, Western media coverage was remarkably consistent in narrative structure: in how it compared the personalities of both victims to the chief suspect, Vladimir Putin; and in its interest in the various conspiracy theories that emerged in the wake of the murders. But what also marks these stories out is the relative absence of prosecution, in other words, calls for a tough response from the West.

The Victims

There was unanimity in the Western media about the virtues of Anna Politkovskaya. The day after her murder, Sunday 8 October 2006, various media described her as: an 'award-winning reporter who fell foul of the Russian authorities for her fearless and critical reporting of the war in Chechnya' (*Sunday Telegraph*); 'The Woman Who Died for Freedom' (*Sunday Times*); 'the most famous reporter in Russia ... lauded by journalists and writers around the world for her exposés in Chechnya' (*Independent on Sunday*); 'the journalist who did most to uncover the Kremlin's dirty war in Chechnya ... a fiery critic of Putin' (*Observer*); and 'one of the country's most prominent journalists' (*New York Times*). As the story developed more fully on the following day, we were told that she

> never wanted to be a war reporter but ended up knowing more about the conflict in Chechnya than any journalist alive. And now she has fallen in battle ... A brave champion of the victims of war (and) unstinting in her campaign to expose the crimes of the powers-that-be.
>
> (*Daily Telegraph*, 9 October 2006)

She was 'a fearless critic of President Putin' (*Times*); a 'reporter loathed by the Kremlin' (*Daily Mail*); 'Russia's most famous and controversial crusading investigative journalist ... Putin's fiercest critic (and) a firebrand for freedom' (*Independent*); 'Russia's bravest and most brilliant journalist' (*Guardian*); and 'the veteran Russian journalist and author who made her name as a searing critic of the Kremlin' (*New York Times*). The oddest description of her came from the *Sunday Mirror* (8 October 2006). It reported that Politkovskaya was 'respected for her critical coverage of the Russian government campaign in Chechnya' under the headline: 'News Girl Shot Dead'.

On the day after the assassination of Boris Nemtsov (28 February 2015), he was reported to be 'a leading opponent of Vladimir Putin' (*Daily Telegraph*); an 'Anti-Putin MP' (*Sun*); 'One of the most prominent and charismatic critics of President Putin ... Charismatic, good-looking and typically dressed in tight-fitting jeans and a casual leather jacket ... a genuinely popular Russian politician ... A brave, authentic and distinctive voice at a time when the country is locked in a dark spiral of war and propaganda' (*Guardian*); 'a liberal politician (who) took the view the economy was on the decline because of the Russian president rather than because of an American conspiracy' (*Independent*). Later that evening, the *Observer* online said he was 'a star politician in the 1990s who was once seen as a potential successor to Boris Yeltsin' who, just hours before his death, 'appeared on a radio programme calling on Muscovites to come out and protest against the economic crisis and the war in Ukraine (and) was working on a report detailing evidence of Russia's involvement in the Ukraine conflict, which the Kremlin denies.'

It concluded that Nemtsov's 'history of opposition to Vladimir Putin [is] seen as most likely reason for death' (*Observer*, 28 February 2015). The picture was completed on the following day, Sunday 1 March 2015. He was the 'Russian dissenter who paid the ultimate price' (*Sunday Telegraph*); and an 'opposition leader ... labelled a traitor' (*Independent on Sunday*). According to the *Sunday Times*, Nemtsov was assassinated just as he was 'poised to embarrass the Kremlin by exposing its role in Ukraine.' There were also personal elegies from friends. In the *New York Times*, the Russian-born journalist, Julia Ioffe, paid tribute to Nemtsov as 'a rising star in Yeltsin-era politics (and) the standard-bearer of Western liberalism.' Although he 'could be a silly bon vivant... he was deeply intelligent, witty, kind and ubiquitous. He seemed to genuinely be everyone's friend' (28 February 2015). In the *Times*, the author and ubiquitous media critic of Putin and his regime, Edward Lucas, declared Nemtsov to have been his 'closest friend in Russian politics' (1 March 2015). He wrote that, 'Bravery, charm, humour and honesty are admirable qualities. But in Vladimir Putin's Russia they mean political oblivion and – in the case of Boris Nemtsov – death'. The *Express* described him as 'The playboy politician brave enough to call Putin "mad"' (3 March 2015).

The Mystery/Conspiracy

In the Politkovskaya case, a headline in the *Independent* (8 October 2006) summed up the murder scene and the first clues:

> Murder in Moscow: a discarded Makarov, pistol of choice for Russian hitmen, and four shells were found next to her body. Evidence that points to the assassination of the journalist who hounded Putin and was about to expose the Chechen PM.
>
> (*Independent*, 8 October 2006)

She had been investigating allegations of torture and kidnapping of civilians by Chechen army officers and held the prime minister, Ramzan Kadyrov, directly responsible. The *New York Times* also saw the abandonment of the murder weapon at the scene as 'the signature of a contract killing' and that the murder 'had the stench of a political assassination' (10 October 2006). In Putin's Russia, it said, 'politically motivated crimes have a way of never being solved.' Its edition the next day reported the emergence of 'alternative theories', some of which suggested:

> a dark conspiracy by the Kremlin's opponents to kill her in order to provoke public protests ... One proponent of that line of thinking seems to be Mr. Putin himself. 'We have information, and it is reliable,' he said in Dresden on Tuesday, 'that many people hiding from Russian justice have long been nurturing the idea of sacrificing somebody in order to create a wave of anti-Russian feeling in the world.'
>
> (*New York Times*, 11 October 2006)

As to the likely assassin, the *Guardian* reported that Russian police were 'hunting a man in a white baseball cap who was filmed by a CCTV camera entering the building a few moments before she was shot three times in the chest and once in the head' (9 October 2006). The *Daily Telegraph* published an image of the man from the CCTV footage, asking, 'Is this the killer of Russian journalist?', and reporting that 'from the Kremlin there was silence. Not even speculation on websites that Politkovskaya's death was a birthday present for Mr Putin, who was 54 on Saturday, the day she was killed, could provoke a government reaction' (9 October 2006).

Mystery and conspiracy also abounded in the reporting of the Nemtsov case, in 2015. The *Independent* reported that, 'Four days after the killing ... the identity, motive and means by which the person, or persons, pulled the trigger on Friday night remain ... shrouded in mystery' (3 March 2015). The headline for the story noted that: 'Kremlin security cameras fail to give clues to Nemtsov murder mystery. No witnesses to assassination but precision of hit "suggests government involvement". The scene of the crime was seen as significant for some in the media. For example, the *Guardian* foreign correspondent, Luke Harding,[2] pointed out that the assassination was carried out:

> within touching distance of the Kremlin and the fantastical bulbous domes of St Basil's cathedral. It is an area infested with police ... yet Nemtsov's killer was seemingly able to escape, having shot his target four times in the chest from a white car ... In the end, Nemtsov fell victim to old-fashioned mafia methods.
>
> (*Guardian*, 28 February 2015)

In the *Daily Telegraph*, Putin critic, Mark Almond, observed that, 'Whoever killed Boris Nemtsov ... had a macabre sense of staging ... [choosing] a famously recognisable backdrop for their brutal elimination of Russia's most prominent pro-Western politician' (2 March 2015).

The style and audacity of the assassination was interpreted by the *Times* as a form of propaganda of the deed. Under the headline, 'Mob Rule', its editorial said it sent out a message that 'critics of the regime are traitors, that traitors deserve to die and that no one is exempt' (2 March 2015). In the *Independent on Sunday*, Dr Michael Pelly, a doctor who once worked in Russia in a humanitarian capacity, wrote that the assassination came at 'a time of increasing talk of nationalism, traitors in our midst and so on' (1 March 2015). For Serge Schmemann in the *New York Times*, Putin may have vowed to bring Nemtsov's killers to justice but the response of some in his administration was telling: 'The authorities have already begun to spin conspiracy theories, including the outrageous suggestion that he may have been killed by political allies to create a martyr' (3 March 2015). The *Guardian* saw this as part of a wider strategy 'designed to confuse those who would seek out the truth with multiple expressions of distracting PR chaff. The tactic is to create as many competing narratives as possible. And, amid all the resultant hermeneutic chaos, to quietly slip away undetected' (4 March 2015).

Having established the credentials of Politkovskaya and Nemtsov as fearless critics of Putin and his administration, and having explored the mystery and conspiracy theories that might explain their deaths, the next task for the media was to investigate the prime suspect behind their murders: Vladimir Putin.

The Prime Suspect

In a feature article that put the assassination of Anna Politkovskaya into the wider context of the risks facing journalists working in Putin's Russia, the *Guardian* stated that 'no one believes (Putin) personally ordered her execution – but there won't be many tears shed inside the Kremlin' (10 October 2006). It is a verdict that summed up the general media approach to guessing who the chief suspect might be: if not Putin, then someone or some agency operating deep within the state apparatus. In an article for the *Independent* (9 October 2006) – 'Putin's Russia failed to protect this brave woman' – Joan Smith wrote about a climate of impunity that:

allows the thugs who target journalists to get away with murder. Forty-two journalists have been killed in Russia since 1992, many in similar circumstances: contract killings, carried out with ruthless efficiency, and for the most part unpunished by the Russian state.

(*Independent*, 9 October 2006)

Simon Heffer guessed that Politkovskaya's critical reporting on the Russian army in Chechnya 'opened up two possibilities about her assassination. Either it was done by a freelance element in the army, angered by her "unpatriotic"' stance on Chechnya, or someone in the government had had enough of her asking difficult questions (*Daily Telegraph*, 11 October 2006). In a similar vein, the *Observer* said that 'her murder will throw suspicion on the security services and the pro-Moscow regime in Chechnya' (8 October 2006). For the *Independent*, even if Putin had nothing to do with the assassination, he could not 'escape political responsibility for a climate in which the law is so readily flouted. Contract killings are no rarity, and those who take a public stand – whether against the Kremlin or corruption – fear for their lives' (9 October 2006).

By the time of Boris Nemtsov's assassination in 2015, the Western media view of Putin had hardened and was less circumspect about pointing the finger of suspicion directly at him. In its editorial of 2 March 2015, the *Daily Telegraph* remarked that, 'Many of (Putin's) most prominent critics have the unfortunate habit of dying, always in circumstances from which the president distances himself.' In an article headed, 'This Means War, Say Kremlin's Critics after Moscow Murder', the *Times* reported the opposition view that 'Nemtsov's assassination marked the beginning of "open war" between President Putin and anyone who opposes him (and) could have been sanctioned only by Mr Putin' (2 March 2015). Another article in the same issue was headlined, 'Street Shooting Makes Putin Look like a Mob Boss Running a Gangster State', and noted 'the widespread perception, inside Russia and overseas, that the opposition politician was eliminated on Kremlin orders' (*Times*, 2 March 2015). But what is most noteworthy here is the extent to which media speculation seemed to take its cue from contributions from staunch Putin critics such as Edward Lucas and Masha Gessen. In an article published in both the *Daily Mirror* (28 February 2015) and the *Sunday Times* (1 March 2015), Lucas wrote that:

> The Putin regime uses force against opponents, whether by murdering, beating or abducting them as individuals ... It dresses up its actions in phoney legalism, and surrounds them with a blizzard of blustering, mendacious propaganda. It uses its grip on power as a means to colossal self-enrichment, and it uses that wealth to bribe and subvert the West. This is bad for Russia and a grave threat to us.

For the *New York Times*, Masha Gessen argued that the assassination was a form of political communication:

> In all likelihood no one in the Kremlin actually ordered the killing – and this is part of the reason Mr. Nemtsov's murder marks the

beginning of yet another new and frightening period in Russian history. The Kremlin has recently created a loose army of avengers who believe they are acting in the country's best interests, without receiving any explicit instructions ... Mr. Nemtsov was gunned down while walking a bridge that spans the Moscow River right in front of the Kremlin. It is under constant camera and live surveillance. The message was clear: People will be killed in the name of the Kremlin, in plain view of the Kremlin, against the backdrop of the Kremlin, simply for daring to oppose the Kremlin.

(New York Times, 1 March 2015)

Now compare these items, in language and tone, to editorials in the *Guardian* and the *Times*. The *Guardian* online, in an article titled 'A Watershed for Russia: This Brazen Assassination Under the Eyes of the Kremlin's Security Cameras Shows the True Character of the Putin Regime', alluded to Stalin's regime when it stated that:

> The killing ... whether it was ordered by Mr Putin directly or not, sheds a harsh light on the nationalist regime fuelled by propaganda that the Russian president has created, a system where the silencing of an independent democratic voice becomes almost a trophy handed to the ruler. Mr Putin has made it a staple of his rule to launch nationwide hate campaigns against those deemed 'traitors' in a way reminiscent of the Stalinist era.

(Guardian, 1 March 2015)

With a similar reference to the Stalin era, headlined, 'Mob rule. Boris Nemtsov's fearless investigation of corruption may have doomed him', the *Times* noted that:

> In Stalin's day, prominent enemies of the state were at least granted a show trial. In Putin's they are shot dead in the street. The murder last Friday night of Boris Nemtsov may never be solved but it confirms with sickening finality that propaganda has taken hold in Russia in the 21st century much as it did in the 20th. It dictates

that critics of the regime are traitors, that traitors deserve to die and that no one is exempt.

(*Times*, 2 March 2015)

It was difficult to find alternative, more nuanced interpretations. With her long experience reporting and analysing Russian affairs, Mary Dejevsky argued in the *Independent* that there were 'easy answers and more difficult ones' to the question of who killed Nemtsov:

The easy answers are: the President, Vladimir Putin – directly or indirectly – because Nemtsov had long been a highly articulate opponent and had recently condemned Russia's policies towards Ukraine ... Yet it would be a mistake to regard Nemtsov's death as any kind of victory for Putin, except in the most primitive sense that a political opponent has been eliminated. The fallout, as the tone of Kremlin statements suggests he at once understood, could be both damaging and dangerous.

(*Independent*, 2 March 2015)

The Prosecution

On the day of Politkovskaya's funeral in Moscow, on 10 October 2006, Vladimir Putin travelled to Dresden, Germany, for a summit meeting with Chancellor Angela Merkel. Looking ahead to the summit, the *Times* noted that the visit to a city that was once part of Cold War, East Germany, marked a return to 'his old haunts from when he was a KGB spy (and) where he tried to recruit moles for the Soviet secret service' (10 October 2006). In these new and very different circumstances, he could expect 'stern words about human rights from the German Chancellor.' On the next day, the paper reported that the murder of the Russian journalist had 'overshadowed the summit, handing ammunition to members of the German political establishment who are resisting closer ties between Berlin and Moscow' (*Times*, 11 October 2006). In an item headlined, 'Putin Faces "Murderer" Taunt as Journalist is Buried', the *Daily Telegraph* reported how he had been heckled on arrival by demonstrators and that the assassination 'forced the Russian leader onto the defensive during a trip that was meant to focus on energy and growing economic ties with Germany' (11 October 2006). In an article headlined, 'West's Muted Response Speaks Volumes', the *Guardian* noted that while the murder

> was condemned by western media and professional and human rights groups ... it provoked a relatively muted official reaction from most western governments. [...] These days most European leaders prefer to appease rather than accuse President Vladimir Putin. Europe's strategically and morally debilitating dependency on Russian oil and gas is one reason. A sense among policymakers that the 'new Russia' is ineluctably going its own unsavoury way is another.
>
> (*Guardian*, 11 October 2006)

The murder of Boris Nemtsov in 2015, just a year after the Crimean crisis, failed to provoke the kind of tough Western response that his supporters may have hoped for. Beyond words of condemnation and platitudes about human rights and democracy, there were no calls for economic or diplomatic sanctions, an absence that was reflected in Western media coverage. However, two items in the media sample were interesting for challenging the generally negative view of Russia and Putin in the reporting of Nemtsov's assassination. In his article for the *Independent on Sunday* (1 March 2015), Dr Michael Pelly argued for a greater understanding in the West of both Putin and his country. Sub-headlined, 'The West's Leaders Show Little Understanding of History, Diplomacy and the Psychology of a Proud Russia Brought Low', the article asked if the West really understood the psyche of Russian people after the collapse of the Soviet Union and the social, political and economic chaos that ensued. A more rounded sense of the Russian perspective was needed for that:

> What is Putin to make of Western leaders who, in fact, seem to have no understanding of history and who blunder into promising, and giving support to countries to whom we have no natural

allegiance? Some Ukrainians want closer links to the West, others to Moscow, but that should be a decision for them. To offer an alliance means a real commitment. Are we seriously prepared to go to war for Ukraine against Russia?

(*Independent on Sunday*, 1 March 2015)

Pelly closed by suggesting that: 'NATO should think beyond Ukraine and try to forge some relationship with Russia … Then we would all benefit from a serious bulwark to protect against future threats that are already on the horizon' (*Independent on Sunday*, 1 March 2015).

On a less forgiving note, the *Guardian* columnist, Seumas Milne,[3] mocked the view of British Defence Secretary, Michael Fallon, that Vladimir Putin was a greater threat to the West than even Islamic State. In a column headlined, 'The Demonisation of Russia Risks Paving the Way for War' (4 March 2015), Milne offered a critique of the West's hostility to the Russian leader that diverged significantly from and implicitly challenged his own newspaper's hostile editorial stance, seen in its most extreme when covering the Crimean crisis in the previous year (see Chapter 5):

There may be no ideological confrontation, and Russia may be a shadow of its Soviet predecessor, but the anti-Russian drumbeat has now reached fever pitch.

And much more than in Soviet times, the campaign is personal. It's all about Putin. The Russian president is an expansion-ist dictator who has launched a 'shameless aggression'. He is the epitome of 'political depravity', 'carving up' his neighbours as he crushes dissent at home, and routinely is compared to Hitler.

Putin has now become a cartoon villain and Russia the target of almost uniformly belligerent propaganda across the western media. Anyone who questions the dominant narrative on Ukraine – from last year's overthrow of the elected president and the role of Ukrainian far right to war crimes carried out by Kiev's forces – is dismissed as a Kremlin dupe.

(Milne, *Guardian*, 4 March 2015)

ESPIONAGE: LITVINENKO AND SKRIPAL

On 1 November 2006, the ex-FSB officer and Putin critic, Alexander Litvinenko, met with two other ex-Russian intelligence agents, Andrei Lugovoi and Dmitry Kovtun, in the Millennium Hotel, London. Within hours after the meeting, he fell seriously ill and was admitted to hospital three days later. He died on 23 November 2006 at which point a post-mortem examination revealed that he had been poisoned by the lethal radioactive substance, polonium-210. Litvinenko had only just been granted British citizenship after seeking asylum in 2000 on the grounds of political persecution. He had published damaging revelations about the FSB, formerly the KGB, including corruption in the agency and a plot to assassinate the oligarch, Boris Berezovsky. He was arrested in 1998 and imprisoned on remand for nine months before being acquitted. However, in 2002, he published a book with Yuri Felshtinsky, *Blowing Up Russia: Terror From Within*, in which he claimed that the FSB was responsible for a series of bombings in Russia in 1999, which were then used as a pretext for the Second Chechen War and to provide a platform for Vladimir Putin's elevation to power. It emerged after Litvinenko's death that he had been working with Andrei Lugovoi on an investigation into links between Spanish crime gangs and the Russian mafia and that he was also a paid agent for the British foreign intelligence agency, MI6.[4]

On Sunday, 4 March 2018, the ex-Russian intelligence agent, Sergei Skripal, and his daughter, Yulia, were found unconscious on a park bench in the English city of Salisbury. At first, they were thought to have been suffering the effects of alcohol or recreational drugs but on admission to hospital their condition deteriorated further, raising concerns that they may have been poisoned. The first police officer to attend the scene of the incident, Sergeant Nick Bailey, fell seriously ill with the same symptoms, while another 48 people were admitted to hospital for medical assessment. The ensuing police investigation revealed that the Skripals had been poisoned by a rare but lethal nerve agent from a group of agents called Novichok; and that traces of the agent had been detected at Sergei Skripal's home and in the pub and Italian restaurant, Zizzi, that he and his daughter had visited earlier that evening. The police also advised anyone who had visited the latter two premises to wash the clothes that they had worn at that time. The Skripals were discharged from hospital weeks later – Yulia in April and Sergei in May – and moved to secure locations. The story of Sergei Skripal's career as a Russian military intelligence officer and how he had come to live in England, offered clues to the police and the media as to why he had been targeted for assassination. In 2006, he was arrested in Russia on charges of being a double agent, passing to MI6 the identities of Russian agents working in European countries and was sentenced to 13 years in prison. But in 2010, he was released as part of a spy swap for ten Russian sleeper agents living in the USA, whereupon he was admitted to live and work in Britain as an intelligence consultant to the British military.[5]

The murder of Litvinenko and the attempted murder of Sergei Skripal (it is still not known if his daughter, Yulia, was deliberately targeted also) had all the ingredients of an old Cold War spy thriller and was constructed as such in the extensive media coverage both cases attracted. As with the reporting of the assassinations of Anna Politkovskaya and Boris Nemtsov, the comparative media analysis that follows is constructed around the metaphor of a murder mystery or crime thriller: the profiles of the victims, the mystery and conspiracies, the identification of the prime suspect, and the response of the prosecution, that is, Western condemnation.

The Victims

News of the death of Alexander Litvinenko on 23 November 2006 was released on the next day and reported by the media on 25 November 2006. He was described as a 'vociferous critic of President Vladimir Putin' and a 'Russian intelligence officer who castigated the Kremlin' (*Daily Telegraph*). He was 'a career security services officer who got sucked into the dark underworld of Russian politics ... a disputed figure; to some a courageous defector and whistle blower, to others a traitor and oligarch's sidekick' (*Guardian*). The *New York Times* described him as a 'former Russian K.G.B. officer and foe of the Kremlin'. The *Sun* struck a rather less sympathetic note when it told readers that Litvinenko 'came from a murky world, and was expert in the same black arts which were used to wipe him out.' He was variously described in the *Independent* as 'a man who could be taught little about the seamy side of modern Russia. A KGB agent for 18 years, he occupied a world where intrigue, betrayal and ruthless trickery were the tools of working life'; a 'middle-ranking Russian security service agent who knew he was risking his life by stepping out of the shadows to go public with accusations against (Putin) the master of the Kremlin' and 'KGB secret agent turned political dissident who lifted the lid on the Russian security services.' An article published in the paper's fourth edition on 24 November was headlined, 'Man with a Life from a Spy Novel' called him a 'former secret agent, political dissident, author, father … a relentless critic of Mr Putin's regime.' The allusion to the spy novel or movie was also made by other media outlets. In an article headlined, 'Red Alert: The Sinister Death of Alexander Litvinenko has Unveiled the Shadowy World of "Londongrad" – a melting pot of dissidents, defectors and billionaire oligarchs', the *Daily Telegraph* said the murder bore 'all the hallmarks of a classic spy novel written at the height of the Cold War'. The *New York Times* reported on 'a day of fast-paced developments that resembled a dark political thriller' (24 November 2006), while the *Daily Mirror* thought the murder scenario 'wouldn't be out of place in a Bond movie' (25 November 2006).

While Litvinenko appeared to be continuing with his challenge to Putin and his regime from his refuge in London, Sergei Skripal was living a much more, low-key existence in Salisbury, although his consultancy work for the British military may have attracted some opprobrium from his former employers back home in Russia. He was described in the media as 'a former Russian intelligence agent (who) had been leading a life of quiet anonymity in Salisbury (where) he was enjoying an unexpectedly peaceful retirement' after being part of 'the biggest spy swap since (the) end of the Cold War' (*Daily Telegraph*, 6 March 2018). The *Daily Mail* reported that he 'was considered by the Kremlin to be one of the most damaging spies of his generation' and described him with the headline: 'The Agent Traded for Femme Fatale' (6 March 2018). This was a reference to

Anna Chapman, one of the ten Russian sleeper agents swapped for Skripal and three other agents in 2010. In every crime story in the popular press, there is nearly always the 'deviant woman' and Anna Chapman, real name Anya Kushchenko, fitted the profile perfectly. Even though she had no other connection to Sergei Skripal, her physical looks and her support for Vladimir Putin were set in contrast to the fate of the former double agent and his daughter. On 7 March 2018, the *Daily Mail*, *Express* and *Daily Star* led with pictures of her on a luxury beach holiday in Thailand and the headlines:

How Spy ... Became Putin's Poster Girl (*Daily Mail*)
The Agent Flaunting her Front on Beach (*Express*)
Agent Anna's Life of Luxury (*Daily Star*)

She was described as a 'buxom 36-year-old redhead ... modelling to eye-popping effect by posting alluring pictures of herself alongside trenchant criticisms of Russia's enemies' (*Daily Mail*); the, 'Flame-haired Russian spy Anna Chapman is flaunting her busty curves on a beach – as Sergei Skripal and his daughter fight for their lives' (*Express*); and the 'Russian spy ... pictured in a swimsuit on a Thai beach while the double agent she was swapped with fought for his life' (*Daily Star*). On these terms, had she been in opposition to Putin, she would most likely have qualified for a favourite tabloid epithet: the 'Bond Girl'.

Other media portraits of Skripal took on a rather surreal dimension when they turned to his lifestyle in Salisbury, a small city, worlds apart from London and the Kremlin. His past as a double agent could have been out of a John Le Carré novel but descriptions of his life in Salisbury read like routine crime reports in a local English newspaper. The *Daily Telegraph* (7 March 2018) reported that, 'The locals at Sergei Skripal's social club hadn't seen the Russian émigré for a couple of weeks' up until the attempt on his life.

The silver-haired, slightly portly pensioner was a Sunday lunchtime regular at the Railway Social Club ... where he would order the roast and wash it down with beer and vodka ... He lived openly in the city and bought a house for £260,000 cash and lived comfortably on an MI6 pension.

(*Daily Telegraph*, 7 March 2018)

The *Daily Mail* referred to him as the, 'Ex-spy in suburbia who joined £10-a-year Railway Club' (7 March 2018). The *Guardian* led with an article headlined: 'Salisbury, Scratch Cards and Sausage: The Quiet Life of Sergei Skripal. Russian spy … seems to be well-liked by locals in Wiltshire town' (6 March 2018). It said that Skripal:

> lived a quiet and modest, but not completely hidden life … Home is a modern red-brick house that he bought under his real name without a mortgage for £260,000 … Skripal, who drives a BMW, shops for Polish sausage at the Bargain Stop convenience store where he also indulges his love of gambling, buying up to £40-worth of lottery scratch cards at a time. He recently joined the Railway social club near the city centre and has developed a taste for local ale as well as vodka.
>
> (*Guardian*, 6 March 2018)

The *Independent* (7 March 2018) described 'the sedate suburban life of a former MI6 double-agent':

> Sergei Skripal certainly didn't look like anyone special. Not for him the ostentation of the London oligarchs, or the high-gated, heavily patrolled Surrey estates of wealthier fellow Russians who had reason to fear Vladimir Putin. No. Mr Skripal preferred the suburban anonymity of a modern brick semi in a quiet little residential estate on the edge of Salisbury. To neighbours, Mr Skripal was the politely friendly if not overly forthcoming gent who was never too flashy, and never that smartly dressed – despite driving a BMW 3 Series. To local officials, Mr Skripal was nothing more exciting than a retired local government planning officer.
>
> (*Independent*, 7 March 2018)

The *Times* reported that in Salisbury, 'Residents called it Smallbury, because nothing ever happened there. Not anymore' (10 March 2018). The town, it said, was a 'perfect refuge for a double agent.' A headline in the *Sun* started with a slightly alarming main title, 'Spy's War Games Exclusive!' before the subtitle revealed something more prosaic: 'The secret life of poisoned spook. Agent's hours playing on PC. Loved guinea pigs & man cave. Riddle of his missing pet cat' (11 March 2018).[6] The *New York Times* (6 March 2018) was similarly fascinated by the humdrum quality of Skripal's existence to the point where it resorted to an old news cliché – interviewing the startled neighbours:

> On Mr. Skripal's quiet street in the west of the town, his neighbors seemed shocked by both the sudden carousel of journalists and by the news that they had been living next to a former Russian spy. 'He was just an ordinary person,' said James Puttock, a 47-year-old scaffolder who lives four doors down from Mr. Skripal. 'I didn't think he was a Russian spy.'
>
> (*New York Times*, 6 March 2018)

The Mystery/Conspiracy

As major media stories, there were two dimensions to the mystery surrounding them. One was the circumstances surrounding the deaths and the possible suspects; the other was the likely weapon used. In the Litvinenko case, the *Daily Telegraph* said that, 'Twist after bizarre twist, the tragic story of Litvinenko's demise has compelled and confused in equal measure' (25 November 2006). In a story headlined, 'I'm Not Vladimir, Says the Third Man', the paper reported on the identity of:

> the mysterious 'Vladimir' who met Alexander Litvinenko for afternoon tea the day he fell ill … Previously described as a figure who was 'tall' and 'taciturn' and who offered Mr Litvinenko tea, Dmitry Kovtun [said] that he was both baffled and angry by attempts to link him to the poisoning … He said the meeting at the Millennium Hotel … was supposed to be about business but they talked

mainly about the weather and dogs. 'I'm known always as Dmitry, never as Vladimir,' said Mr Kovtun.

(*Daily Telegraph*, 25 November 2006)

The *Times* reported in a similar vein even down to the headline allusion to Cold War fiction: 'Poison Case Turns to Hunt for Third Man' (23 November 2006). The *Guardian* headlined its editorial of 25 November 2006: 'Alexander Litvinenko: A Still Mysterious Death', while the *Independent* featured a 'Q&A' headlined 'Deathbed Accusations, Furious Denials, and Key Questions Surrounding Spy's Death' (25 November 2006). The *Daily Mirror* commented that, 'Defections, clandestine meetings, hit-lists and allegations the Kremlin was behind his assassination is the sensational stuff of Cold War espionage ... This is the murky world of emigre politics at its most impenetrable' (25 November 2006). And the *New York Times* said that 'the circumstances leading to the death ... remained murky and confused' (24 November 2006).

Until the results of the autopsy examination, the exact cause of Litvinenko's death was also subject to media mystery and speculation. The *Times* reported that, 'Doubts persist over whether the substance used to attack Mr Litvinenko was the toxic metal thallium, or something else' (23 November 2006). The *Guardian* referred to 'a mysterious poison which has baffled doctors' (24 November 2006). And in similar but rather more vernacular terms, a headline in the *Daily Star* declared: 'Docs Baffled as Poison Spy Fights for Life' (24 November 2006). The *Sun* said that 'Litvinenko was taken ill after having lunch with a pal at a sushi bar in the capital,' but that 'Mystery still surrounds the exact cause of death' (24 November 2006). Another item in the same issue reported that, before his death, Litvinenko had speculated that his food at the restaurant had been laced with the poison, Thallium. The paper described the substance as 'colourless, odourless and tasteless. A bit like sushi, then.' However, the *Daily Mirror* reported that 'Doctors and police yesterday ruled out speculation that the heavy metal thallium was to blame and also said that radiation poisoning was unlikely' (24 November 2006).

The *Guardian*'s online edition (24 November 2006) was among the first in the media to report the official cause of death as confirmed by the Health Protection Agency: radiation poisoning by a high dose of polonium-210. The paper's print version reported on the next day on the 'unprecedented public health scare' that ensued. The *New York Times* reported how 'alarm spread across London after the police found traces of radiation in three places the former spy had been: a sushi bar, a hotel and his North London home' (25 November 2006). It also provided a detailed description of the poison and its potency:

> Polonium 210 is highly radioactive and very toxic. By weight, it is about 250 million times as toxic as cyanide, so a particle smaller than a dust mote could be fatal. It would also, presumably, be too small to taste. There is no antidote, and handling it in a laboratory requires special equipment.
>
> (New York Times, 25 November 2006)

An excited toxicologist told the paper: 'This is wild! To my knowledge, it's never been employed as a poison before ... That's going to be something like the K.G.B. would have in some secret facility or something' (*New York Times*, 25 November 2006). In what is now standard fashion, the popular press in Britain, which used to be called 'the tabloids', sensationalised the nuclear scare with headlines on 25 November 2006, such as:

> Nuked: Spy Killed with Radioactive Poison (*Daily Mirror*)
> Death Spray (*Sun*)
> Sushi Bar's Nuke Alert (*Daily Star*)

A similar pattern of reporting emerged when the media speculated about what happened to the Skripals in Salisbury, 'the city infected with fear [in a] once peaceful suburbia of John Betjeman's imagination' (*Daily Telegraph*, 10 March 2006). Some media reports pointed back to those that surrounded the death of Litvinenko:

> ... there are many similarities with the assassination of Alexander Litvinenko on the orders of the Russian government in 2006. (*Express*, 7 March)

Echoes of Litvinenko Affair ... (*Guardian*, 6 March)
... the case drew immediate comparison to the murder of ... Alexander Litvinenko (*Independent*, 6 March)
Another Litvinenko? ... Woman also critical as police look for links to 2006 case (*Independent*, 6 March)

The speculation focused on what the substance that infected them was:

Was Deadly VX Nerve Agent Used in Attack in Salisbury? (*Daily Telegraph*, 7 March)
The case drew immediate comparison to the murder of former FSB officer Alexander Litvinenko using radioactive polonium-210 (*Independent*, 6 March)
Was It Polonium? (*Sun*, 6 March)

... and on how it had been administered without their awareness:

Was He Sprayed in the Street? (*Daily Mail*, 7 March)
Nerve agent may have been inside gift (*Times*, 8 March)
The nerve agent (was) more than likely sprayed in their faces in an aerosol attack, experts believe (*Daily Mirror*, 8 March)
Spy Poison 'In Parcel' (*Sunday Express*, 11 March)

The *Times* considered alternative, less frightening possibilities. The Skripals 'could have suffered an accidental drug overdose or been struck down at the same time by a sudden but non-suspicious illness. They could have been attacked, but not by a foreign state' (7 March 2006).

It was not until 11 March that the British government was able to ascertain what the substance actually was: one of a group of 'military grade' nerve agents called Novichok, described in the *New York Times* as: 'The nerve agent too deadly to use, until someone did' (13 March 2006). Unlike polonium-210, which has to be ingested to be effective, the Novichok agent can be ingested, inhaled or absorbed through the skin at which point it works to break down the nervous system leading to respiratory or heart failure. In the case of the Skripals, doctors were able to intervene to save them, using antidotes such as atropine or athene, which help to stop the lethal action of the agent. In a mysterious footnote to the case, in June 2018, a couple, Charlie Rowley and Dawn Sturgess, from nearby Amesbury, came into contact with Novichok; it was contained in what they took to be a bottle of perfume. Rowley survived the contact but Sturgess died on 8 July.[7]

The identification of a Novichok nerve agent as the cause of the Skripals' illness triggered predictable panic and anger in Salisbury and in the media when the information was released. The panic was a response to lethal potential of the agent to kill hundreds of people:[8]

Cause for alarm? (*Daily Telegraph*)

Panic in poisoned city (*Daily Star*)

De-contaminate! Hundreds warned in spy toxin alert (*Daily Mirror*)

Lethal newcomer to a covert war (*Daily Mirror*)

Pub & car checks in spy toxin probe (*Sun*)

Nerve agent Novichok 'destroys your mind and body, even if you survive' (*Independent*)

Novichok among the world's most deadly chemical weapons (*Daily Telegraph*, 13 March)

Nerve agent can claim victims for many years (*Times*, 14 March)

The anger was directed at the government and security agencies for their slowness to make the identification public:

Officials face nerve agent backlash (*Daily Telegraph*)

Why did they take a week to warn us? (*Daily Mail*)

Why did it take so long to raise the alarm over health threat? Fury over the week-long delay to warn the public (*Express*)

Expert criticises lack of information. Residents back view of chemical weapons specialist who accuses authorities of being blindsided (*Guardian*)

Diabolical how we've been kept in dark (*Express*, 13 March)

Salisbury residents angered by 'slow' Government response to spy attack (*Independent*, 14 March)

The Prime Suspect

In the wake of Litvinenko's assassination in 2006, media suspicions that it was on the order of Vladimir Putin were tentative to say the least, lacking anything based on substantial evidence. A report in the *Times* headlined, 'Kremlin's Denials Fall Flat', asserted that 'Russia's repeated denials that it was involved in the poisoning of Alexander Litvinenko has done little to ease concerns that the Kremlin remains ready to use force abroad against its enemies' (23 November 2006).

The *Daily Telegraph* interviewed the two ex-KGB officials who met Litvinenko at the hotel. The first was a gentleman called Andrei Lugovoi who told the paper he was the 'victim of a plot by unknown people to frame him' (24 November). The other suspect, Dmitri Kovtun, told the newspaper on 25 November that he was 'baffled and angry by attempts to link him to the poisoning' in a story headlined, 'I'm not Vladimir, Says the Third Man'. In its editorial that same day, the *Daily Telegraph* admitted that:

> *There is, as yet, no evidence linking the poisoning of Alexander Litvinenko to the Kremlin.* While many commentators believe that there is a connection ... hearsay does not constitute proof. We do not know for sure that Mr Litvinenko was murdered and, if he was, the deed may have been done by his ex-KGB colleagues acting without higher authority (emphasis added).

The *Daily Telegraph* was right to admit to the lack of evidence in the case but, as we shall see, its warning that 'hearsay does not constitute proof' that the killing was officially sanctioned appeared to go unheeded in most other sections of the British press.

The *Times* reported that, 'Britain's intelligence agencies last night claimed that the poisoning of the Russian dissident Alexander Litvinenko bore the hallmarks of a state-sponsored assassination' (25 November 2006). *Daily Mail* columnist, Ann Leslie, commented that 'when the man accused of murdering Litvinenko is the Russian

President Vladimir Putin, this bizarre killing cannot be dismissed as a "just fancy that" news story' (25 November 2006). According to the *Guardian*, Labour government ministers were 'said to be "dreading" the possible repercussions of a public inquest into Mr Litvinenko's death, at which they expect his associates to make damning accusations against the Russian government' (25 November 2006); while the *Independent* warned that a Putin connection 'could lead the frostiest relations between Russia and Britain since the height of the Cold War' (25 November 2006). In comparison, suspicions about Putin's involvement in the attempted murder of Sergei Skripal, in 2018, were much more heightened. This may be explained by the enmity and confrontation between the West and Russia over the war in Ukraine and, especially, Russia's annexation of the Crimea in 2014 (see analysis of media coverage in Chapter 5), which seemed to copper fasten the enemy image the Western media did so much to construct.

The *Daily Telegraph* revealed that:

Vladimir Putin vowed to kill the Russian double agent poisoned on British soil (declaring) that 'traitors will kick the bucket' ... The emergence of Mr Putin's warning will reinforce ministers' belief that the attack on Col Skripal in Salisbury was state-sponsored and perpetrated by the FSB Russian intelligence agency.

(*Daily Telegraph*, 7 March 2018)

Russian specialist and regular contributor to media content on Russia, Mark Almond, argued in the *Daily Mail* that, amid the speculation as to who tried to kill Skripal, 'one thing is certain that Vladimir Putin is intent on bolstering his status at home while sowing confusion and dissent across the West ... relentlessly wooing potential allies in his attempt to destabilise the big Western institutions' (7 March 2018). On the following day, the same paper reported that, 'Putin attacked Western sanctions against his country, saying we will win in the long run' and issuing the chilling warning: 'Those who serve us with poison will eventually swallow it and poison themselves' (*Daily Mail*, 8 March 2018). And the *Daily Mail*'s columnist and former war correspondent, Max Hastings, called Putin 'a gangster worth £20 billion running a gangster regime [with a] licence to commit the most appalling atrocities – which he gets away with because the West always blinks first' (10 March 2018). The *Express* decided that, 'While it is too early to say beyond a shadow of a doubt that the Russian Federal Security Bureau is involved in the poisoning of Sergei Skripal, it is certainly looking that way' (7 March 2018). In a guest column for the paper, Frederick Forsyth, author of the assassination thriller, *Day of the Jackal*, told readers that:

> the attempt to kill Sergei Skripal and his daughter was a carefully planned contracted hit [and that] inside Russia no one would dare for one moment undertake such a contract killing without the personal sanction of the man at the very top: Vladimir Putin … For him there are no limits to Russia's vengeance as Salisbury last Sunday proved.
>
> (*Express*, 9 March 2018)

For the *Sun*, 'Putin's henchmen were desperate to take revenge on Sergei Skripal after he gave MI6 the identities of hundreds of Russian agents' (6 March 2018). In its editorial on the following day, headlined, 'A Toxic State', the paper declared: 'This is not the work of a legitimate member of the international community. Other nations do not send assassins to Britain. It is the work of a gangster state we have treated with timidity for too long' (*Sun*, 7 March 2018). The *Guardian* decided that:

> the attack on Skripal looks more likely to belong to the category of hits organised and approved by the Russian state. And given the long political fallout of the Alexander Litvinenko murder, it is unlikely that intelligence agencies would risk such a gambit without a signoff at the highest level.
>
> (*Guardian*, 7 March 2018)

In the *Independent*, Andy McSmith saw the attempt on Skripal's life as a warning from the Kremlin that 'nobody escapes the long arm of

Vladimir Putin's revenge' (7 March 2018); and in the newspaper on the next day, the headline: 'Sophistication of Toxin Suggests Links to State Sponsors' (8 March 2018). For the *Daily Mirror*, failure to 'bring a suspect to court in this case ... will be frightening evidence of the Kremlin's reach' (7 March 2018). And in an exceptional insight into the Russian perspective on the incident the *Independent* reported that 'the story was initially met with stony silence on most state publications. Later on Tuesday, that silence was replaced by angry accusations of "phobia", "hype" and "hysteria"' (7 March 2018).

The Prosecution

What was remarkable about the assassination of Litvinenko – carried out in a major Western capital using radioactive material – was the very muted international response, including from the media. The *Daily Telegraph* reported an EU meeting in Helsinki, with Putin in attendance, in which 'Mr Litvinenko's death went unmentioned in six hours of talks' (25 November 2006). Its editorial that day – headlined, 'The West is Losing Patience with Putin' – complained that:

> Until now, the West has tended to overlook Mr Putin's authoritarianism, largely for the sake of a quiet life. But there must come a point when our patience runs out. It is one thing to tyrannise your people; quite another to presume to do so on British territory.
>
> (*Daily Telegraph*, 25 November 2006)

In the same issue, columnist Simon Heffer asked:

> Is Russia licensed to kill in London? Does our Government, which lives in fear of the tyrant Putin because of his control of so much of our future energy supplies, propose to protest about the Kremlin's new habit of sending its murderers to our capital city to kill people with whom it has a quarrel? Or is there, where dear Vlad is concerned, an acceptable level of assassination?
>
> (*Daily Telegraph*, 25 November 2006)

In an article for the *Times* headlined, 'The One Way to Fight Putin's Menace', Edward Lucas wrote that, 'Speedy justice, efficient government and public-spiritedness are lacking in Russia – and just what we need to make our system envied at home and abroad' (25 November 2006). The newspaper itself reported that 'Mr Putin has been deeply embarrassed by the murder. His open quest to make Russia respected again around the world is not helped by accusations of running a gangster state' and urged that:

> Any policy of trying to tough it out should be met with an even tougher response from Britain. Mr Litvinenko was a citizen of this country. His murder is an affront to our laws, our democracy and our way of life.
>
> (*Times*, 25 November 2006)

The *Daily Mail* columnist, Ann Leslie, said that: 'We have not only imported into Britain the New Russians with their extravagant tastes for champagne, caviar and call-girls, but also the darker, feral, endemically criminal aspects of all that new wealth now coursing through our capital city' (25 November 2006).

Newspapers on the centre-left of the editorial spectrum were just as low key in calling for action. The *Guardian* limited itself to reporting anxieties among Labour government ministers about the likely repercussions the assassination might have for Anglo-Russian relations with headlines such as, 'Foreign Office Fears for British–Russian Relations' and 'Ministers Fret that Rift with Russia will Widen' (25 November 2006). Beyond that, neither the *Guardian* nor the *Independent* offered a strong editorial position. However, the *Daily Mirror* offered a slightly more nuanced view when it argued that Britain was right to demand cooperation from Russia in bringing Litvinenko's assassins to justice but also noted that while

> Putin's regime has suppressed internal opposition and was shamefully allowed to wage a brutal war in Chechnya with barely a peep of protest from western countries ... Britain is also home to groups

who ripped off Russia when Communism collapsed and what can only be called mafia gangsters from the old Soviet state.

(Daily Mirror, 25 November 2006)

When it came to the attempted murder of Sergei Skripal, the response was very different. For the most part, the media response to suspicions that the Russian state was ultimately responsible for the attempt on Skripal's life generated much more extensive and hostile content. Perhaps this can be explained by the fact that relations with Russia had steadily worsened in the intervening years since the murder of Litvinenko and that the Skripal case had happened against the backdrop of recent events such as the Crimean crisis in 2014, and also the impending Russian presidential election, just a week away, and the forthcoming World Cup 2018, which was to be held in Russia. This can be analysed according to three distinct themes that emerged from the coverage: calls for a boycott of the World Cup by the Royal family, the government and even the England team; calls for tough economic and diplomatic sanctions; and the media reporting of and reaction to the official government position once the use of Novichok was confirmed on 12 March 2018.

World Cup Boycott

In a sample of 399 media items, 23 focused on calls for a boycott of this major tournament in 2018 as a means of hurting and humiliating Russia. Of these, 18 came from right-of-centre newspapers, with eight from the *Daily Mail* (for the full list of headlines, see Appendix B). Most of this sub-sample, about two-thirds of the total, focused on the boycott proposal as pushed by the Foreign Office or, more precisely, the Foreign Secretary, Boris Johnson. For example:

> Foreign Office suggests UK might consider withdrawing officials and dignitaries from World Cup (*Guardian*, 6 March)
> I'll give Vlad a World Cup kicking. Johnson warning to Putin (*Daily Star*, 7 March)
> Boris has a sanction in mind for Russia – England to boycott the World Cup (*Independent*, 12 March)

World Cup boycott would hit Putin hard (*Daily Mail*, 10 March)
World kicks off over the Vladi footie. Mass cup boycott urged
(*Daily Star*, 10 March)
Speculation mounts over World Cup boycott (*Daily Telegraph*, 13
March)

The *Daily Star* reported the view of one of the suspects in the assassination that: 'The sanction Russia fears most following the poisoning
of Sergei Skripal is a World Cup boycott' (12 March 2018); and the
Daily Mail led with a threat that might not have frightened Vladimir
Putin as much as the newspaper seemed to suppose: 'England's
WAGs (wives and girlfriends) are set to snub World Cup (*Daily Mail*,
8 March 2018).

The focus on the role of the royals, especially Prince William,
honorary President of England's Football Association (FA), came
from the centre-right media. On the surface, an England football
boycott of the World Cup might have seemed a rather impotent, even
ludicrous, propaganda response to an enemy assault on the nation.
On the contrary, it holds an emotional and psychological potency
that works on the same persuasive level as advertising. As all the
major world powers of history have realised, the most effective propaganda does its job by appealing to the common, the ordinary and
the symbolic. Football, *the* national game. Football, *the* game of the
common people. England, led by Tottenham Hotspur's Harry Kane
– English yeoman and warrior – heading into the ultimate sporting
tournament, the World Cup. The St George's flag, the anthems, the
Second World War chants and songs. Only, in 2018, the tournament is hosted by Russia, a country whose intelligence agents have
just carried out yet another hostile act on home soil (Remember
Litvinenko, 2006?). But the team needs a leader to take them into
battle and there is a distinct reluctance on the part of the players
and manager to surrender this chance to be stars on the world
stage. The country needs leadership and inspiration in this moment
of footballing crisis. It needs a Shankly, a Busby or a Ferguson (all
Scots). Step forward William and Harry, sons of Diana, the 'people's
princess'. Step forward these princes of the English Lionhearts:

Will Royals now snub World Cup? (*Daily Mail*, 7 March)

Wills & Harry could boycott World Cup after Boris threat (*Daily Mirror*, 7 March)

Duke and Prince have 'no plans' to cheer on England side in Russia (*Daily Telegraph*, 8 March)

William planning to stay away from World Cup (*Times*, 8 March)

Official: William will snub Russia's World Cup as spy row rages (*Daily Mail*, 8 March)

William 'not going to the World Cup' (*Express*, 8 March)

William's World Cup visit could be in doubt if proof of Russian poison plot emerges (*Telegraph*, 7 March)

The British government finally announced on 14 March 2018 that, along with members of the Royal family, no minister of any rank would attend the tournament in an official, representative capacity. However, the debate was reheated a week later against the backdrop of the Russian presidential elections with the near certainty that Putin would be re-elected for a fourth term. This related to calls to widen the boycott to include the national squads of England, France and Germany, a move ex-Chelsea FC executive, Christian Purslow thought would be 'hugely damaging for Vladimir Putin's regime' ('Put Boot in with Footie Boycott', *Daily Mirror*, 20 March 2018). In the *Independent*, the journalist, Ian Burrell, said he would not attend the tournament but follow it instead on television (19 March 2018). Yet, at the same time, he advised the top presenters and pundits to 'read up on international diplomacy as much as on VAR goal line technology [and] be wary of being played in Putin's World Cup game' (*Independent*, 19 March 2018). The *Daily Star* reported that: 'Safety fears sparked by crazed Russian Ultras, a war of words among politicians and a wave of anti-British sentiment means that requests to FIFA have plunged by 75% compared to the tournament in Brazil' (20 March 2018). But, as the headline summed it up, no such fears would deter die-hard England fans: 'Putin's Spies, Yobs & Safety Fears Won't Stop our Lionheart Fans' (*Daily Star*, 20 March 2018).

Among the very few dissenting voices were the *Sun* columnist, Tony Parsons, and the England manager, Gareth Southgate, who opposed the idea of a boycott. Parsons lampooned the earnestness that underwrote the boycott campaign. Under a headline that punned on Prince Harry, 'Harry Up and Call a Boycott', he remarked that: 'We learn that Prince William and Prince Harry will not be attending the World Cup in Russia. Ooh, I bet that has them quaking in their furry boots in the Kremlin' (*Sun*, 11 March 2018). And with its typical penchant for a bad pun, the paper led with the headline: 'Men V Boycott. Southgate: We Must Go to Moscow' (*Sun*, 11 March 2018). In the end, William and Harry followed the boycott script, while Southgate prevailed. He led his team to Russia, with a following of fans and media commentators and pundits who enjoyed themselves immensely. And, as with the build-up to the war in Iraq in 2003, the anti-Russian propaganda in the wake of the Skripal poisonings failed to take hold. In 2003, the majority of Western public opinion simply did not believe what they were being told. In 2018, 'the footie' came first, a priority that was perhaps gazumped by the top team of the tournament: the World Cup 2018's corporate sponsors. The line-up was impressive: Budweiser, Hisense, McDonald's, Vivo, Adidas, Coca-Cola, Wanda, Kia, Qatar Airways, Visa and the Russian gas giant, Gazprom.[9]

However, there was a right-wing media chorus of demands for a much tougher government response than just a World Cup boycott. In its editorial on 7 March 2018, 'Cold War Flares Up Again', the *Express* opened with the apparently wise advice that: 'We are deep in Cold War waters here and it's time we reacted proportionately'. Yet, it concluded on a rather shriller note when it urged that 'we cannot allow this state of play to continue. [...] This thuggery must stop' (*Express*, 7 March 2018). With a lack of irony, the *Sun* complained in its editorial on the same day, 'A toxic state', that Russia's

warplanes, ships and submarines provocatively encroach into our waters and airspace. It has launched cyber warfare to destabilise the West. It bankrolls Syrian slaughter. It invaded Ukraine and stands accused of shooting down a jetliner. All the while its gangland criminals launder their millions in London.

(*Sun*, 7 March 2018)

In response, it said, 'we must hit back with economic, political and diplomatic aggression of our own. And crack down on the Russian thugs using our capital as their playground' (*Sun*, 7 March 2018). As the following sample of headlines illustrates, the clamour for a tougher response was widespread and sustained, with a cue again from Boris Johnson:

Boris Wades into Russian Spy Case (*Independent*, 7 March)

Furious Boris Gets Tough with Mad Vlad (*Sun*, 7 March)

We Must be Ready to Stand Up to Russia (*Daily Telegraph*, 7 March)

Use of Rare Chemical Raises Pressure on UK To Take Tough Steps Against Kremlin (*Daily Telegraph*, 8 March)

May Faces Calls to Break Off Diplomatic Ties After Attack (*Times*, 8 March)

Tame Hostile Russian Bear (*Express*, 9 March)

Punish Putin (*Sun*, 9 March)

Let's hit Putin Where it Hurts – in the Pocket (*Sunday Times*, 11 March)

Hit Putin Where it Hurts – in his Wallet (*Mail on Sunday*, 11 March)

Mrs May Must Show Russia that She is an Iron Lady Too (*Sunday Times*, 11 March)

Corrupt Russians Face UK Visa Ban (Sunday *Telegraph*, 11 March)

An editorial in the *Sun*, 'Turn Off Vlad TV' (10 March 2018), urged the government to target the Russian broadcaster, RT (formerly, Russia Today), and remove its licence to operate in or transmit to the UK. This was an idea promoted by Edward Lucas in the *Times* (9 March 2018). In an article headlined, 'We're All Bark and No Bite ... Britain talks a tough game about Russian meddling in our affairs but fails to take the action necessary to stop it', he put forward a number of measures Britain could take but focused particularly on RT, which he called 'the Kremlin's glitzy propaganda outlet'. Without contributions to 'its puppet-show broadcasts' from British journalists and politicians, and without funding from British advertisers, he argued,

'RT would be an unwatchable freak show, featuring only conspiracy theorists, cranks and useful idiots' (*Times*, 9 March 2018). Another anti-Putin pundit, Mark Almond, contributed to hostilities with an item for the *Daily Mail* headlined, 'Britain's Only Got Itself to Blame for Putin's Gangsters on our Streets' (7 March 2018). He warned that unless Britain and its allies imposed tough sanctions on Russia, then 'Putin's response will be to carry on with the same gangsterism and there will be more poisonings to come' (*Daily Mail*, 7 March 2018).

The liberal-left press was much more divided over the appropriate response to the crisis. The *Observer* featured two items that favoured the 'get tough' approach, with the headlines: 'Softly-Softly Isn't Working. Time to Play Hard with Russians in UK'; and, 'If the case against Russia is proved, charge Putin with the attempted murder of Sergei Skripal. The Salisbury poisoning is a brazen attack on a sovereign country and cannot go unpunished' (11 March 2018). The *Guardian* and the *Independent*, on the other hand, adopted a much more sceptical stance with particular reference to the political fallout of the Brexit referendum in 2016. The *Guardian* said that while 'Mrs May can and must stand up to Russia's bullying regime. She must hope also that the UK's European neighbours are minded to stand with her' ('Sergei Skripal and the sowing of discord', 9 March 2018). In its editorial on 7 March 2018, the *Independent* said that 'with Brexit fracturing longstanding friendships and alliances, Britain's "robust" response doesn't amount to very much.'

There were only a few examples of more nuanced, even critical commentary on Britain's response to the Skripal poisonings. In an article headlined, 'Britain would not win a spy showdown with Putin … A hawkish response will get us nowhere', the *Guardian*'s security correspondent, Richard Norton-Taylor, wrote that 'the British government should calm down and encourage British intelligence officers to start engaging with their Russian opposite numbers', an approach he thought would see Russia take Britain more seriously (6 March 2018). Three days later, the paper's columnist, Simon Jenkins, pointed to what he described as the 'sheer hypocrisy' of Britain's outrage over the attempted murder of a Russian citizen on British soil while its armed forces were carrying out drone strikes against targets in Syria (9 March 2018). In the *Mail on Sunday*, Peter Hitchens mocked the official and rather hawkish official response (11 March 2018). In a column headlined, 'We're Goading Russia into a Dirty War We Cannot Win', he pointed out that:

> We are not morally perfect ourselves, with our head-chopping aggressive Saudi friends, our bloodstained Iraq and Libyan adventures, and our targeted drone-strike killings of British citizens who joined IS. But we also have no real quarrel with Russia. We have made it up out of nothing, and now we are losing control of it.
>
> (*Mail on Sunday*, 11 March 2018)

It took eight days for the British government to respond officially to the Skripal poisonings. Prime Minister Theresa May told the Commons, on 12 March 2018, what the mysterious agent was and how her government was going to respond. Having being briefed in advance, the media dutifully reported the official line that morning:

> May poised to blame Moscow directly for nerve agent attack (*Daily Telegraph*)
> May set to hit back at Russia over spy death (*Times*)
> May to blame Russia over poison spy today (*Daily Mail*)
> 'Russia to blame for Salisbury' (*Sun*)
> May 'to blame Russia for spy attack' (*Daily Mirror*)

Her statement at the dispatch box in parliament included a 24-hour deadline to President Putin to explain evidence that Russian agents were involved and that the Novichok nerve agent was traceable only to Russian state laboratories. This tough-sounding language of the ultimatum and the deadline was picked up in the headlines of the popular press the next day:

> We've Vlad enough: PM's ultimatum to Russia Putin gets 24hrs to explain poison plot (*Sun*)
> Nailed by Novichok ... May blames spy murder bid on Putin (*Sun*)
> May gives Putin 24 hours to tell us truth (*Express*)

Putin blame on Russians: May's deadline to Kremlin (*Daily Star*, 13 March)

This was promoted as the most fitting response to be taken against Russia as a 'rogue nation' (*Times*) and 'Putin's gangster state' (*Daily Mail*). The *Sun* reported that the Prime Minister's statement of blame would 'plunge relations between London and Moscow to their lowest since the Cold War' (12 March 2018) and that the 'Cold war heating up over poisoning' (13 March 2018); while the *Times* (14 March 2018) feared that in an 'unstable world' the Skripal crisis was 'unfolding against a backdrop of the most serious threats to western democracies since the Cold War.' The *Express* (12 March 2018) was somewhat more definitive: Britain was now 'Fighting a new Cold War'.

Yet the problem here was that the prime minister's statement avoided mention of specific measures that might be taken against Russia, leaving some in the media to fill the vacuum. Writing in the *Daily Telegraph*, the former Conservative leader, William Hague, said that in this moment of national crisis, it was 'time for apologists to recant, optimists to become realists, and pacifists to slink away' and for the West 'to show strength and resolve in the face of unacceptable behaviour' (13 March 2018). The *Times* took its cue from the Russian opposition leader, Alexei Navalny, who told the paper that a World Cup boycott or removing RT's licence to broadcast in the UK would 'play into Putin's hands' (14 March 2018). He called on the British government instead to 'Kick Russian tycoons out of country to really hurt Kremlin'. With the headline, 'Punish Putin', the *Sun* said that Britain's 'European allies and America should stand alongside us with measures of their own to cripple this gangster regime once and for all. That would wipe the smirk off Putin's face' (12 March 2018). And in a long article for the *Guardian*, the diplomatic editor, Patrick Wintour, proposed 'an escalating list of potential measures', from one to ten in order of severity depending on the seriousness of Russia's response (12 March 2018). These can be summarised as follows:

1. Expulsion of diplomats;

2. Ask Ofcom to declare that Russian media outlets such as RT are not fit to hold a broadcasting licence;

3. Seek support in the EU for sports officials not to attend the World Cup;

4. Introduce amendments to the sanctions and anti-money laundering bill;

5. Freeze assets of Russian oligarchs;

6. Seek further EU-wide sanctions on Russia;

7. Step up NATO presence on the Russian border;

8. Designate Russia as a state sponsor of terrorism;

9. Cut Russian banks off from Swift; and

10. Leak or publish classified material on the scale of alleged money laundering by Putin and his allies.

(*Guardian*, 12 March 2018)

Only the *Independent* (13 March 2018) warned against the dangers of overreaction. In an editorial headlined, 'May has pointed the finger … now she must decide what action to take,' the paper said that:

> the Prime Minister must balance her righteous anger – which will be shared by many – with a demonstrable understanding that not all Russians (either in Russia or living elsewhere) can be held directly responsible for the actions of the Russian state. She mustn't create national bogeymen.

(*Independent*, 13 March 2018)

Yet, the story did not finish there. Police linked the attempted murder of the Skripals with the mysterious death of Dawn Sturgess, in Amesbury, just months later in July: they were caused by the same Novichok nerve agent, contained in an aerosol perfume bottle with a luxury brand name. Given that Amesbury was on the train route from Salisbury to London, the circumstances all pointed to a developing police theory. On 5 September 2018, the police released more detail. There were two suspects, going by the names of Alexander Petrov and Ruslan Boshirov, which police believed to be false aliases, and who were in fact senior officers of a Russian intelligence agency. On the basis of a close circuit television trail of their movements from arrival in the UK to Salisbury, twice, and back to Russia, the police charged the suspects in absentia but knew that it was unlikely they would ever return to the UK to face trial and possible conviction. A week later, on 12 September 2018, the pair appeared on the Russian television channel, RT (formerly Russia Today), for an extraordinary interview in which they gave their version of events.

Before looking at the media response to their version, it is worth recapping it on their terms in the parodic style of the British television comedy panel game, *Would I Lie to You?* Here, members of opposing panels tell an apparently unlikely story and challenge their rivals to decide if it is true or false. This is not to make light of the death of Dawn Sturgess and the near-death of her partner, Charlie Rowley; or to show disrespect to the Skripals and all those others affected by the assassination attempt. Rather, it is to crystallise the cold contempt shown by Petrov and Boshirov to the whole episode. They knew they were lying, they knew that most people watching knew they were lying but they also knew they were not going to face criminal justice for what they had done. That sheds some light and shadow on the media coverage of the episode: how worthy the response was, yet also how hopeless and futile.

SPIES LIKE US

Petrov and Boshirov appeared on RT to deny any part in the alleged plot to kill Sergei Skripal and explain that they had travelled to the UK as tourists. They only had a few days so it was important to take in some of the great tourist attractions on offer. Not Buckingham Palace, or Big Ben and the Houses of Parliament, or the Tower of London and Tower Bridge, not even the Victoria and Albert Museum and Tate Modern. Instead, they took a train to the small city of Salisbury in Wiltshire, just a 90-minute train journey, south-west of the capital and site of their big attraction: Salisbury Cathedral. Not only had it a fine, 123-metre high spire and a working fourteenth-century clock but it also happened to host an original

copy of the thirteenth-century Magna Carta, the historical significance of which today is hotly disputed. Also disputed was the reason
why they carried with them a bottle of high-end fashion perfume.
Clearly taken aback by the revelation and, in the spirit of investigative journalism worldwide, the interviewer pressed them further.
Why would two Russian men travel to England, ignore London, and
travel south to see Salisbury Cathedral with a bottle of perfume? The
men side-stepped the question and went on to tell her how a shower
of sleet forced them back to London but that they returned to Salisbury the next day to complete their visit, before then heading back
to Heathrow to catch their flight back home. After the show, the presenter took to Twitter to muse on the perfume lead. Were these men
gay? The replies confirmed her suspicions. Two men with perfume?
Of course, they must be gay and, because gay men were prohibited
from the armed forces, they could not possibly be military intelligence and therefore must be as they claimed: two 'decent lads' on
holiday.

The story provoked incredulity and derision in the British press.
Some newspapers led with the official response from 10 Downing St:

> No 10 calls Salisbury suspects' interview 'blatant lies'. Downing
> Street says pair's claims they were tourists are 'insult to public's
> intelligence' (*Guardian*, 13 September)
> May: Salisbury denial is an insult to our intelligence (*Daily Tele-
> graph*, 14 September)
> Insult to our intelligence. May dismisses Russian TV circus as
> 'deeply offensive' (*Daily Mail*, 14 September)

But the focus of coverage on 14 September 2018 was on the likeli-
hood of the suspects' story:

> The unlikely tale of two tourists who simply came 'to see Salisbury
> Cathedral' (*Daily Telegraph*)
> Lies, damned lies and lies you don't expect anyone to believe
> (*Times*)
> Come off it, comrades! Ten glaring flaws that blow a huge hole in
> their version of events (*Daily Mail*)

We just wanted to visit Britain to cut loose and have some fun say
Russian poisoners (*Express*)
We're not spies we're tourists! Novichok suspects in 'ridiculous'
TV claim (*Daily Star*)
Two 'decent lads' visiting the cathedral: Russian suspects on their
Salisbury trip (*Independent*)
You're Putin it on ... Novichok assassins say they travelled from
Russia 'to see Salisbury's Cathedral clock' (*Daily Mirror*)
Dreaming of spires and Novichok – in the footsteps of Salisbury
sightseers (*Sunday Times*, 15 September)

In the *Independent* (14 September 2018), parliamentary sketch
writer, Tom Peck, sent up the story in a piece headlined, 'Terrible
Weather Then Wanted for Murder – the Russian Holiday from Hell':

[N]ever did two Russian men not only have their short weekend
using London as a base to explore Salisbury by train ruined with
snow, the bad weather making it simply impossible for them to be
among the 1,200 or so people who somehow still managed to visit
Stonehenge that day, but six months later their miserable weekend
would also land them in the firing line for the most internationally
notorious murder and attempted murder in decades. Ordinarily,
this is the sort of thing that would end with at least a strongly
worded letter to the tour operator, but in the absence of such a
possibility, a sit down interview with your country's state backed
TV channel will have to do.

(*Independent*, 14 September 2018)

However, the media narrative largely followed the same pattern
shown in each of the case studies in this chapter: that the trail of
evidence always ends at the door of Vladimir Putin and his regime.
In the *Daily Telegraph*, Jonathan Eyal, Director of the Royal United
Services Institute, mocked the claims of the suspects and he argued
that 'this bizarre story tells more about Russia itself than it tells about
us. And it clearly has no connection with the truth' (14 September
2018). In an item in the *Times* headlined, 'Lies, Damned Lies and

Lies You Don't Expect Anyone to Believe', Michael Binyon explained the cynicism behind Putin's denials, referring to a special word (in Russia), *vranyo*, 'meaning to tell a lie that you do not expect anyone to believe but that is told purely to save face … [It] deceives no one: the person telling the lie knows that the person listening is absolutely sure that this is untrue but will not challenge this untruth' (14 September 2018). The *Daily Mail* described the whole episode as, 'Putin's brazen two fingers to the world … so blatant they'd be laughable – if what they revealed about Russia's leader wasn't so chilling' (14 September 2018). Writing in the *Express*, Bill Browder charged that:

> While Russia is full of criminals and dishonest officials, there is one thing which is clear and consistent. And that thing is that everybody is afraid of Vladimir Putin. They are all afraid of him because if you cross Vladimir Putin in any way, at best you'll lose your job, at worst you'll be killed.
>
> (*Express*, 13 September 2018)

Elsewhere, the RT interview with 'Putin's liars' (*Sun*) marked 'a new low in [the Kremlin's] war of words' (*Sunday Express*, 16 September 2018). Jonathan Freedland's column in the *Guardian* was headlined, 'Russia's Brazen Lies Mock the World … The RT interview was risible. But Putin's attempt to dismantle the truth is deadly serious' (14 September 2018). However, the *Sunday Telegraph* (16 September 2018) published an item that appeared to offer an alternative explanation of the RT interview. Sourced to 'Whitehall officials', this was that Petrov and Boshirov were in fact victims of a feud between Russian intelligence agencies and that the men were being punished for leaving such a careless trail of evidence in their wake as they headed back to Russia after the attempt on Skripal's life.

CONCLUDING REMARKS

As this chapter has shown, the media coverage of the assassinations of Anna Politkovskaya, Boris Nemtsov and Alexander Litvinenko, along with the attempted murder of Sergei Skripal, all followed the narrative structure of a murder mystery but with elements of the Cold War thriller. And they all identified President Vladimir Putin as the prime suspect, based on the assumption that, in each case, only he, as Russia's ultimate power, could authorise such ultimate sanctions. However, Mary Dejevsky suspects that, since Litvinenko's assassination, this kind of framework has not been cutting through to wider public opinion:

> There has been quite a divergence between the views expressed by successive UK governments and the media on the one hand, and the views of 'ordinary people' on the other. For instance, you find a lot of contesting views if you read the 'below the line' comments even for such papers as the *Daily Mail*, and in social media, where people question the very hard line taken by the government and the article they are commenting on. I have found the same, when taking part in radio phone-ins. Also university-age audiences tend to be quite sceptical of the official government/media line on Russia. So the actual influence exerted by government/media views may have started to be counterproductive. There was an enormous amount of scepticism over the Skripal case, which has only really been silenced by the total clamming up of government spokespeople and the highly selective release of information.[10]

Chapter 5 analyses Western media coverage of four military interventions by Russia under the leadership and direction of Vladimir Putin: the first phase of the Second Chechen War (1999–2009), the Russo–Georgian War (2008), the annexation of the Crimea (2014) and the military support of the Assad regime in the Syrian War, from 2015.

5

Putin at War:
From Chechnya to Syria

On 12 June 1999, a unit of 200 Russian troops, based in Bosnia as part of the UN Peacekeeping force, moved into Kosovo just as the war there ended. It was a bid to reassert Russia's right to play a peace-keeping role in Kosovo after having been snubbed at the war's outset. The unit beat the much larger NATO contingent in a race to the capital, Pristina, and occupied Slatina Air Base at Pristina International Airport. If anything, it was something of a propaganda coup for Russia and highly embarrassing for NATO. Its military commander on the ground, US General Wesley Clark, adopted a hard line on the Russian initiative and ordered British General, Mike Jackson, to block any attempt by Russian aircraft to land at the airport, by force if necessary. Jackson defied the order, telling Clark, 'Sir I'm not going to start World War III for you'. He preferred to set aside his anger and meet the Russian commanding officer to negotiate a way out of the confrontation ('Sneaky Russians Leave Big Mike Smouldering', *Independent*, 14 June 1999). The Western media dramatised the story within an old Cold War framework:

NATO Faces Russians at Pristina (*Independent on Sunday*, 13 June)

NATO Goes In: Russians Warned (*Observer*, 13 June)

Call Off Your Mad Dogs, Yeltsin: Clinton's Warning as Russians Refuse to Allow NATO Forces into Airport (*Sunday Mirror*, 13 June)

NATO Troops Roll into Kosovo: Confusion Over Russian Move (*New York Times*, 13 June)

Russia Celebrates at the Expense of Humiliated NATO (*Times*, 14 June)

In Britain, the *Times*, the *Daily Mail*, the *Guardian* and the *Independent*, all alluded to the Red Army's push for Berlin at the end of the Second World War. Under the headline, 'Shades of 1945 in the Russians' Advance', the *Times* reported that:

Russia's coup [in Kosovo] recalls the deadly rivalry 55 years ago in the race for Berlin [and] prompted Western fears that the Russian forces, like the Red Army, may be the prelude to the partitioning of Kosovo. In the dying days of the Second World War, the race between General Patton and Marshal Zhukov to reach the Third Reich's capital marked the start of the Cold War that lasted half a century.

(*Times*, 12 June 1999)

In the *Independent*, Anne McElvoy recalled how the Soviet Union 'proved unfailingly adept at seizing the photographic offensive and adapting it to its propaganda needs', specifically in this case to push its narrative that 'the clash between Russia and Germany, not the fate of the rest of Europe or the defeat of a vile dictator, had been at the heart of the [Second World War].' In a similar way, the race to Pristina 'was intended to reassure a desperate population that Russia can still be first at something' (14 June 1999). This was perhaps a rather blunt interpretation of Russia's motives because it neglected the depth of resentment the country felt about being sidelined during NATO's Kosovan operation and its sense of trauma and humiliation following the collapse of the Soviet Union and its status as a superpower. As it happened, the confrontation at Pristina airport was resolved quickly, with an agreement that the Russians could after all maintain their own peacekeeping force in Serbian sectors of the country. However, the incident presaged a new era of more serious conflicts in which, under the leadership of Vladimir Putin, the Russian military directly intervened in defiance of Western condemnation and the imposition of economic sanctions.

This chapter will take as detailed case studies the media coverage of: the first phase of the Second Chechen War (October 1999–February 2000); the Russo–Georgian War (2008); the annexation of the Crimea from Ukraine (2014); and, in 2015, Russia's military backing for President Assad in the Syrian Civil War (2011–). Each case study will show how the coverage was defined by the media framework, 'Putin versus the West'.

THE SECOND CHECHEN WAR (FIRST PHASE, OCTOBER 1999–FEBRUARY 2000)

The Second Chechen War began formally with the invasion by Russian forces on 1 October 1999. The conflict was defined by a military phase that lasted until the end of February 2000 and an insurgency phase that was to last until 2009. Estimates of total military/civilian deaths and disappearances in the ten-year conflict vary wildly between Russian, Chechen and international human rights sources. Amnesty International puts the toll at 25,000,[1] while less reliable sources put it as high as 200,000.

The initial tipping point for Russia and Prime Minister Vladimir Putin appeared to be the invasion in August 1999 of the neighbouring Republic of Dagestan by two armies totalling nearly 2,000 men and led by Chechen militant, Shamil Basayev and Saudi mujahedeen commander, Ibn al-Khattab. The majority of the men were Chechen but also included an international contingent of Islamic militants and mercenaries. The Russian army succeeded in pushing them out of the Republic by mid-September but a series of bombings and hostage-takings in Russia outraged public opinion and gave Putin a legitimate excuse to order an outright invasion of Chechnya to finally defeat what he defined as a terrorist threat to Russian national security. Although there were suspicions and conspiracy theories among Putin's political opponents as to who was really responsible for the bombings – Chechen militants or Russian intelligence officers – Putin enjoyed broad public support for the invasion, in its initial phase at least. His rhetoric about the humiliation that Russia suffered during the disastrous First Chechen War, 1994–1996, played well to wider nationalist sentiment in the country. During that conflict, he was director of the intelligence service, then called the Federal Counterintelligence Service (FSK). By its very nature, as the successor agency of the KGB, this had a very low-profile role with little in the way of public awareness or accountability. Now, as prime minister in 1999, Putin's reputation and political survival were very much front and centre of how this new conflict in Chechnya would play out in Western news coverage. This case study covers the first, military phase of the war, that is, the initial invasion (1–31 October 1999; based on a sample of 110 newspaper items); and the assault and occupation of the capital city, Grozny (1 December 1999–31 January 2000; based on a sample of 440 newspaper items). The analysis focuses on Putin's image, his propaganda war with a hostile West, and the degree to which the Western media defined it within a Cold War construct.

Putin

Chapter 3 of this book showed how the negative image of Vladimir Putin in the West was established from his first term as Russian President, 2000–2004, and has continued to his latest in 2018: as first and foremost an ex-KGB officer but also a narcissist, hungry for attention, public acclaim and international respect. Yet, the seeds of that image can be seen in the media construction of the man as prime minister and key driver behind the Second Chechen War effort. In a profile of Putin for the *Independent* – 'Russia's Avenging Angel' – Helen Womack wrote that:

> When Vladimir Putin speaks about Chechnya, his ice-blue eyes light up with an inner fire … In four months he has gone from a dry and derided little nobody to … favourite for president next year. …There is something frightening about the simmering anger, even fanaticism, that he hides only just beneath his smooth, cool surface.
>
> (*Independent*, 12 December 1999)

The *Times* admitted that:

> like the party that supports him, little is known about this former spy and judo black belt. Fit, smart, energetic and ruthless, he has

cultivated an image of a man not afraid to take difficult decisions, whatever the diplomatic or military costs might be.

(*Times*, 21 December 1999)

The ultra-conservative *Daily Mail* emphasised Putin's image as 'Russia's hardline premier' (15 December 1999) and 'the hard man on course to rule Russia' (21 December 1999).

In the first weeks of the war, the elite liberal press in the West reported the invasion of Chechnya as being all about President Putin. On the one hand, they acknowledged the level of support he was enjoying as a strong, decisive prime minister in sharp contrast to the increasingly erratic and infirm President, Boris Yeltsin:

> Mr Putin's best chance to enhance his image among voters is by acting decisively against the threat of terrorism. In the last fortnight his popularity rating has doubled to 48%.
>
> (*Guardian*, 1 October 1999)
>
> [Putin's] poll ratings as President Yeltsin's apparent heir have risen during the crisis.
>
> (*Times*, 2 October 1999)

By late October, the *Times* reported that his ratings had 'shot up to an extraordinary 70 per cent' (20 October 1999). The *New York Times* also quoted this rating and another poll in which '32 percent said "will and determination" were Putin's dominant traits' (*New York Times*, 21 October 1999), while the *Independent* claimed that 'Two-thirds of Russians agree he was right to send the army into Chechnya' (24 October 1999). Many of the newspapers explained Putin's popularity as being the result of a carefully manufactured (but high-risk) ploy in a broader political strategy. He was keen to use the Russian media to project an image of himself as a strong, decisive leader and action man. Putin, holding crisis meetings; Putin, talking tough about terrorism; Putin, flying a fighter jet into Chechnya to survey the progress of his army; Putin, standing up to the West. This new prime minister had his eye on a bigger prize: the presidency of the Russian Federation, with the next election only months away in

March 2000. The *Guardian* was particularly strong on this theme in the first weeks of the invasion. Its leader on 7 October 1999 – 'Russia's Gamble: Ceasefire in Chechnya Before It's Too Late' – declared that:

Putin, an old KGB hand, is an ambitious fellow. He knows that his wish to succeed President Boris Yeltsin would be boosted by a credible claim to have vanquished the 'black'[2] Chechen terrorists, held responsible for recent bombings in Moscow and elsewhere, and to have regained national territory. He has used fear, anger and popular prejudice to maintain a domestic consensus challenged, at present, only by liberal [opposition]. But one man's reckless career plan does not constitute a policy. In truth, Russia is taking an enormous gamble.

(*Guardian*, 7 October 1999)

Later in the year, the paper described him as 'the master of chaos and this calamity suits his sorry purpose' (*Guardian*, 9 December 1999); 'Without a party, or political history,' it said two weeks later, 'Mr Putin needed to establish himself as a leader. He needed a national crisis' (*Guardian*, 21 December 1999). When President Yeltsin resigned on New Year's Eve and Putin stepped in as acting president, the paper observed that:

His breath-taking ascent from obscurity to the role of acting president … may not be exclusively due to the war in Chechnya, but that has clearly been its most powerful ingredient. Indeed, promoting Mr Putin, may be what this second Chechen war is all about.

(*Guardian*, 3 January 2000)

The *Times* noted that:

Sceptics in Russia and abroad may make comparisons with the film *Wag the Dog*, in which a US president cynically declares war on a remote land to save his re-election bid. But even if such conspiracy theories are still mulled over in Russian kitchens, they cut ever less ice with the voters who must choose a new President next June when Boris Yeltsin retires.

(*Times*, 20 October 1999)

Yet as the military campaign progressed, with mounting civilian casualties, the liberal Western press in particular preferred the conspiracy theory that this was Putin's war, one that he used to promote his own political ambitions. A photo-feature on Putin in the *Times* highlighted:

a certain nostalgia for the 'strongman' in Moscow. For Putin read Stalin. But there may be an even stronger sense of nostalgia for Uncle Joe among Chechens. He may have deported them, but better a ticket to the gulag than a bullet in the kulaks.

(*Times*, 21 December 1999)[3]

A profile in the *Observer* by Amelia Gentleman – headed 'Vladimir Putin: Vlad the Inheritor' – said that 'Putin looks like a man in control of his destiny, basking in the successes of his main political project, the war in Chechnya' (12 December 1999). The *Daily Mail* spoke of 'the Kremlin hardliner nicknamed the Grey Cardinal' (19 December 1999); and when President Boris Yeltsin resigned on 31 December 1999, to be replaced by Putin in an acting role until the next election, Russia expert Owen Matthews compared the two men:

Vladimir Putin could not be more different from the erratic ruler he replaces. While Boris Yeltsin has always been a volatile maverick, Putin is a man of the system, a conformist and a bureaucrat to the bone. Yeltsin is a hard drinker prone to depression; Putin is straitlaced, calm and almost frighteningly self-controlled. Yeltsin is verging on senility; Putin is a trim 47-year-old who enjoys showing off his prowess at judo. And whatever his failings, Yeltsin is loaded with that indefinable Russian quality, *dusham* (soul) whereas Putin is as colourless as a winter evening in Moscow.

('The Colourless Insider who is Wildly Popular',
Daily Mail, 1 January 2000)

On the following day, the *Mail on Sunday* featured a profile of Putin by Mark Almond,[4] headed, 'This Unknown may be Another Stalin':

Putin always appears calm and in control. Perhaps his KGB training taught him how to lull suspects into a false sense of trust before pouncing all the more effectively. Looking like a villain out of a James Bond film, he has a sinister charm and that indefinable quality that gives some leaders a hold over people just like a snake with rabbits ... [if] anyone can emulate the Peter the Greats or Stalins of Russia's past, her new, coldly calculating and ruthless leader is the man.

(Mail on Sunday, 2 January 2000)

The *Observer*'s profile – 'Action Man Putin Casts Aside Yeltsin's Legacy. Russia's New Leader Rouses Troops in Chechnya and Looks like an Election Winner' – said that:

The new Russian strongman's five months as Prime Minister are bathed in Chechen blood. And in one of his first acts as Acting President yesterday, [he] went to the war that has been the key to his dizzying rise to power.

(Observer, 2 January 2000)

Another facet of this media construction of Putin as the Russian hard man and war leader was his interactions with the West: political leaders, governments, and international institutions and organisations.

The West Responds

In the early invasion phase of the war, the Western response was muted, limited only to calls for Russia to be cautious and to avoid the disastrous mistakes of the First Chechen War of 1994–1996. The *Times* remarked that 'such blandishments will carry little weight in Moscow, which is still smarting from being pushed to the side-lines during NATO's air war over Kosovo' (1 October 1999). But as the invasion progressed with mounting civilian casualties and a refugee crisis, liberal sections of the Western media became more critical of what they saw as Western inaction. The *Independent* in Britain was foremost in campaigning for effective Western intervention. Its editorial of 11 October 1999 declared that:

> The world's main reaction to the horrors now unfolding in Chechnya has been little more than a shrug of collective shoulders ... Outright condemnation of the mayhem unleashed by the Russians in Chechnya is not just desirable. It is essential. Chechnya Mark I was bad enough, with its civilian massacres. But at least Russia and the West alike seemed to have learnt the lessons. Chechnya Mark II is a nightmare too far. The rest of the world must say so.
>
> (*Independent*, 11 October 1999)

Yet, by the end of October 1999, the paper had to admit that: 'Any direct intervention by the West which threatened that assumed pre-eminence would bring us into confrontation with a nuclear-armed state with the power of veto at the United Nations' (*Independent*, 29 October 1999). In its editorial on 7 December 1999, the *Guardian* found itself facing the same contradiction between the principle of intervention and the reality of its implications. Headlined, 'The West Must Take a Stand on Chechnya', the article excoriated the 'vacuous pronouncements' of European leaders but admitted that, 'Nobody wants to risk a military confrontation with nuclear-armed Russia over Chechnya ... Chechnya is not Kosovo, and Russia is not Serbia. Much as some might wish it, we cannot send in the smart bombers.'

The critical turning point for the West came in late November 1999, when Russian forces laid siege to the capital, Grozny, with a campaign of aerial and artillery bombardment. The end goal was to drive out Chechen militants by completely destroying the city with the use of aerial bombing raids and multiple rocket launchers armed with thermobaric or fuel-air explosives. Although at this point, most civilians had fled the city, up to 40,000 still remained, most of them too elderly or infirm to leave on their own. On 5 December 1999, the Russians ran leaflet drops, urging them to leave by 11 December

1999 or face certain death. The ultimatum was greeted with outrage in the West and condemned by human rights organisations as a war crime. Some media headlines spoke of Western 'warnings' and 'rebukes' to Russia but the majority highlighted the limitations and powerlessness of the response:

> War crimes are being committed in Chechnya every day. And still we look away (*Independent*, Leader, 8 December 1999)
>
> Impact of World Outrage will be Limited (*Times*, 8 December 1999)
>
> World powerless to stop bombing as Moscow defends ultimatum given to Chechen capital (*Guardian*, 8 December 1999)
>
> The West may wish to halt the Russian advance but it cannot (*Guardian*, leader, 8 December 1999)
>
> The West Does What it Can: Not Much (*Guardian*, 9 December 1999)
>
> EU Leaders 'Powerless' to Stop Russian Blitz (*Independent*, 9 December 1999)

In a parliamentary debate in Britain, on 7 December 1999, the Foreign Secretary Robin Cook argued for Europe to impose swingeing economic sanctions against Russia as its invasion continued to take heavy civilian casualties:

> Cook warns Russians (*Guardian*, 8 December 1999)
>
> Cook: We'll Cripple Russia (*Express*, 8, December 1999)

However, a satirical, parliamentary sketch by Matthew Parris in the *Times* (8 December 1999) was rather more scathing, undermining the Foreign Secretary's stance.[5] Under the heading, 'Rocket Robin Bombs the Russians with Adjectives', Parris mocked the outrage vented by Cook and other MPs with the use of a military metaphor:

> The trigger for the Foreign Secretary's fearless attack was Question 21, from a Conservative backbencher, Laurence Robinson (Tewkesbury), whose assault on Russian misbehaviour in Chechnya may

become known as the Tewkesbury Raid ... The Foreign Secretary flew the first sortie himself. This was a high-level drop and Mr Cook had armed himself with the full thesaurus. Jets blazing, he roared across the Central European skies. Bombs away! 'Wholeheartedly condemn'. Bam! 'Deplore'. Crump! Far below, we could see Russian installations ablaze already. 'The planned visit of the OSCE,' growled Cook, his jet banking into a steep curve, 'may now be pointless.' Kerthump! A thin plume of black smoke rose from now-devastated conference facilities at the Kremlin. Cook came back for another assault: a stonker. If Russia were to proceed with the expulsion of civilians from Grozny, he barked, EU leaders might 'review the next tranche' of funds promised to Russia for modernisation. Review? Wham. The next tranche? All of it? Ouch. Take that, Ivan!

(*Times*, 8 December 1999)

While the West was portrayed as powerless and limited, Russia was depicted as confident in its conduct of the Chechen campaign and contemptuous of Western attempts at diplomatic intervention:

France, Germany and Italy issued a joint statement expressing their 'deepest concern' at the bombing campaign. But Moscow's foreign minister, Igor Ivanov, said it was an internal Russian affair.

(*Guardian*, 1 October 1999)

Russian ministers yesterday snubbed offers of European Union mediation ... determined to refuse any offers of help from outside.

(*Times*, 8 October 1999)

Europe's foreign relations supremo Chris Patten was snubbed by the Kremlin. His plea for Russia to accept mediation was rejected before he even had the chance to put it on the table.

(*Express*, 8 October 1999)

Putin gave an icy rebuff to Bill Clinton ... effectively telling him to mind his own business.

(*Independent*, 8 December 1999)

Kremlin Snub for Peace Move (*Express*, 16 December 1999)

Putin Snub For Truce as Grozny Is Pounded (*Express*, 18 January 2000)

Putin Ignores Peace Appeal (*Independent*, 29 January 2000)

In a remarkable article for the *Times* on 3 December 1999, just two days before Russia's controversial ultimatum to the civilian population of Grozny, Putin explained his war policy in Chechnya with reference to the Irish peace process and the Good Friday Agreement, signed in the previous year. In the article headlined, 'Why We are Fighting in Chechnya', he applauded the negotiations towards a settlement and the end of violence in Northern Ireland but refuted the idea that the war in Chechnya might be settled by a similar process of mediation on the basis that: 'Grozny bears a far greater resemblance to the anarchy and terrorism of Beirut in the 1980s than it does to Belfast in 1999.' There could be no negotiating with terrorists, he went on.

> To ask the Russian Government to negotiate a settlement with these vicious criminals is tantamount to asking Peter Mandelson and George Mitchell to broker a peace deal with Manchester's drug barons or crime bosses in London. Such a notion is unthinkable.
>
> (*Times*, 3 December 1999)

What Putin seemed to forget about the Good Friday Agreement was that the British government had in fact negotiated with terrorist or paramilitary groups towards a ceasefire in their respective campaigns; initially in secrecy, in the late 1980s, but then through a kind of media, or megaphone, diplomacy into the early 1990s, which led to the Downing St Declaration of the British and Irish governments in 1993 and the paramilitary ceasefires in 1994 (McLaughlin and Miller, 1996; McLaughlin and Baker, 2010). A few days after publishing Putin's article, the *Times* reported that Britain's Minister for Europe, Keith Vaz, had rejected comparisons between Chechnya and Northern Ireland; while an unnamed government official remarked that: 'We did not bomb Belfast' (8 December 1999). Whether the article was written by Putin himself or by an advisor is open to question but it was certainly an unusual departure for a leader and a government that usually communicated to the Western media via official spokespersons or direct statements. In fact, it appears to fit with a new Russian public relations or propaganda strategy in wartime that bears similarities with NATO's tactics during its air war in Kosovo, only a few months previously, in April 1999. And it was picked up on by some sections of the media that feature in the sample for this case study.

The Media and Propaganda War

Media journalism is now a prominent feature in the coverage of major Western conflicts since the Vietnam War: journalists reporting on their relationships with militaries and government officials as they attempt to media manage a particular campaign.[6] My study of these relationships during the Kosovo conflict (McLaughlin, 2002) found a clear difference of attitude among the British media pool attached to NATO headquarters in Brussels from colleagues reporting on the ground in Serbia and Kosovo and in the television studios in London. In Brussels, the majority of journalists seemed happy to consume without question the information they were given during the daily military briefings, coordinated by the NATO press secretary, Jamie Shea. They appeared to accept the NATO version as true and transparent rather than one filtered by information management and public relations: in other words, propaganda. Robert Fisk of the *Independent* travelled to NATO HQ and challenged both NATO's version of the air war he was reporting on the ground and the media pool's acceptance of it. He called the journalists, 'sheep in wolves' clothing' but was dismissed by Shea as suffering from 'an excess of moral perfectionism' (McLaughlin, 2002: 26).

Such was the success of NATO's media war in Kosovo that Russia was to adopt the same tactics during the Second Chechen War. The state still imposed an information blackout and it still excluded journalists from the war zone; but when the civilian death toll began to rise above 'acceptable levels', Russian public opinion began to turn against the war, and it set up a new, centralised information agency called the *Rosinformcenter*. This employed the very same 'warspeak' used during the Kosovo conflict. The *Times* correspondent, Giles Whittell illustrated the immediate effect of the new strategy:

> Whatever it looks like, Russia's second war with Chechnya is against 'terrorists', not Chechen fighters. It has produced no 'refugees', only civilians driven from their homes by bandits ... although air raids continued over much of Chechnya yesterday, they did not deliver 'precision strikes' ... instead, Russian aircraft are carrying out 'strikes aimed at the annihilation of the infrastructure and manpower of international terrorists'.
>
> (*Times*, 21 October 1999)

In an excoriating critique of the approach for the *Independent* – 'Moscow Gets NATO Bug – and Civilians Die' – Robert Fisk noted that since Kosovo, NATO warspeak was being adopted by the USA and Israel to smooth over civilian casualties during operations in Iraq and Lebanon respectively:

> And now it's the Russians who are NATO's copycats, bombing Chechnya with 'precision', seeking only 'military targets' and 'the total elimination of terrorist bases' – the same hopeless aim of Israel's regular onslaughts against Lebanon. And, of course, the war is going wrong. Russians are dying, civilians are dying, apparently by the hundred.
>
> (*Independent*, 11 October 1999)

Fisk's colleague for the same newspaper, Patrick Cockburn, doubted that the new approach was changing hearts and minds among the Chechens or critics in Russia as 'official spokesmen continue to issue heavy-handed propaganda suggesting that the Chechen fighters are demoralised and that Chechen civilians welcome the Russian army ... but any sympathy for Moscow is likely to be diminished by the bombing of towns and villages' (*Independent*, 26 October 1999).

The Second Chechen War was to turn into a long insurgency. It lasted until 2009 and included Chechen terrorist attacks on Russian territory, for example, the Moscow theatre hostage crisis, 23–26 October 2002, halfway into Putin's first term as Russian President. The siege ended with a controversial security operation that took the lives not just of the Chechen group but also 130 of the hostages, who succumbed to a gas used by the Russian anti-terrorism team. However, criticism of the Putin administration both in Russia and internationally was muted because it was able to point to the aftermath of 9/11 and the USA's 'war on terror' as justification. But Russia's brief invasion of and war with Georgia, in 2008, was against an internationally recognised state and drew a very different response from the West and the Western media.

THE RUSSO–GEORGIAN WAR (2008)

Russia's war with Georgia in 2008 was, like the two Chechen wars, the outworking of long simmering ethnic conflicts exacerbated by the dissolution of the Soviet Union in 1991. Although it is widely known as the 'Russo–Georgian' War, it also involved the two self-declared republics of South Ossetia and Abkhazia. Both have majority populations of ethnic Russians and both have resisted Georgia's long-held claim over them as part of its sovereign territory. The conflict was also fuelled by the mutually hostile relationship between Vladimir Putin, now prime minister, and the American-educated, pro-Western Georgian president, Mikheil Saakashvili. Saakashvili had been lobbying the USA to support his bid for membership of NATO and the EU. For Russia, with its decades-long fear of Western military encirclement, to have a NATO country right on its border and with territorial waters in the Black Sea was unthinkable.

On 7 August 2008, Georgian troops invaded South Ossetia, after Ossetian militia shelled Georgian villages amid ongoing tensions between the two territories. In a counter-offensive, Russian troops invaded South Ossetia and Georgia on 8 August and Abkhazia, via the Black Sea Fleet, on 9 August. A ceasefire agreement, brokered by French president, Nicolas Sarkozy, was reached on 12 August

2008. Although Russia formally recognised the independence of the disputed republics, it did not complete the withdrawal of troops from Georgia until 28 August 2008. This was a sign, many thought without concrete evidence, of Putin's determination to teach Saakashvili a lesson not to mess with Russia or even to destroy his political credibility as president. Casualty figures in this brief war vary between Russian, Ossetian and Georgian sources but they were minimal compared to the slaughter that marked Russia's wars in Chechnya. The conflict caused significant civilian displacement, with movement between Russia, Ossetia and Georgia, estimated by Amnesty International at around 192,000 people.[7]

The media analysis that follows is based on a sample of 490 news items over a sample period of 6–20 August 2008. It will focus on the portrayal of Putin as a war leader and his relationships with Saakashvili and Medvedev; the West's response to the conflict and Russia's reaction; and the role that public relations played in shaping Western perceptions of the protagonists.

Putin

The established enemy image of Putin was front and centre of the media coverage of the Russo–Georgian War. He was the 'former KGB man who was skilled in making it appear he was an adversary's friend' (*Daily Telegraph*, 11 August 2008); and one whose 'action man persona transmitted a determination to prevail' (*Sunday Telegraph*, 13 August 2008). According to the *Times*, Putin was 'Tsar Vladimir' or, quoting the *Wall Street Journal*'s epithet, 'Vladimir Bonaparte' (17 August 2008). He was, 'A bullying beast' (*Daily Mail*, 11 August 2008). A *Sun* editorial called him 'Brutal Putin ... a bully boy ... bent on using Russia's vast military machine to grind tiny Georgia into the dust' (12 August 2008). His invasion of Ossetia and Georgia was 'a ruthless display of brute power' (*Guardian*, 16 August 2008). The *London Independent* and *New York Times* were more measured in their references to Putin, preferring instead to see the conflict in terms of Russia, its motives and strategy, rather than through the personality of its prime minister.

According to the Russian constitution, the office of prime minister is subordinate to that of the president and comes with a portfolio of responsibilities that is confined to domestic policymaking. The responsibility for the foreign affairs lies chiefly with the office of the president. When Putin stepped down after two terms as president in May that year to allow for the election of his political ally, Dimitry Medvedev, the new president appointed him prime minister. The Western media were quick to decide that Putin was by far the real power. He was the 'puppet-master' and Medvedev the 'puppet' (see Chapter 3). In an item headed, 'Russia's Ruling Voice: Vladimir Putin', the *Sunday Telegraph* had 'little doubt about who was in charge at the Moscow end. Russia may have had Dmitry Medvedev as its president since May, but it was his hawkish predecessor, Vladimir Putin, who appeared to be calling the shots' (10 August 2008). Reporting for the *Times*, Mark Franchetti said that the war in Georgia answered 'the question that world leaders have been asking since Vladimir Putin stepped down as President this year: who runs Russia? The answer, of course, is Mr Putin' ('Putin Leads From Front to Send US a Bullish Message', 11 August 2008). Two days later, the same newspaper compared how the two men were handling the conflict, including the hostile international reaction. The headline read: 'The Puppet Medvedev is Left Dangling by an Action Man Called Putin' (*Times*, 13 August 2008). A profile of the prime minister as war leader by Owen Matthews in the *Daily Mail* (12 August 2008) was headlined, 'Revenge of the Puppet-Master: No Longer President but Still Pulling all the Strings, Putin is More Dangerous than Ever'. Matthews opened by declaring that there was 'little doubt that Vladimir Putin still wears the trousers in the Kremlin.' Medvedev might 'technically be' president, he continued, 'but when the bullets began flying in South Ossetia last week, it was to Putin that Russia and the world looked for answers' (*Daily Mail*, 12 August 2008). While Putin 'radiated resolve and natural authority ... undignified Medvedev, by contrast, could barely conceal the fact that he was badly out of his depth leading his country into war' (*Daily Mail*, 12 August 2008). For the *Independent*, Putin was 'still the real power' in Russia (9 August 2008), while President Medvedev 'looked positively uncomfortable in his public appearances' since the start of the war, Putin was 'in his element' and 'clearly back in the driving seat – if he ever vacated it' (12 August 2008).

Saakashvili

The West's view of Georgia's president, Mikheil Saakashvili, was divided and sometimes internally conflicted between official statements of support and unofficial anxieties about his personality and behaviour. This was clearly evident at NATO's annual summit in Bucharest, Romania, just four months previously (2–4 April 2008), when Georgia and Ukraine asked to join NATO's MAP or Membership Action Plan. European members, particularly Germany, France and the UK, argued that the issue was not *if* Georgia and Ukraine should be admitted to the MAP but *when*. As things stood, they had serious reservations about admitting the two countries in the face of Russian opposition (Putin was in attendance at the summit as one of his last official duties as outgoing president of Russia). And they were very suspicious of Saakashvili, whose provocations of Russia over South Ossetia might lead NATO into direct, potentially cataclysmic, confrontation with Russia. The USA was officially in support of Georgia's right to be admitted but its State Department expressed private reservations, fearing that it would alienate Russia, whose support the USA needed in its campaign to stop Iran developing its alleged nuclear weapons plan.

Such reservations went back further again to 2004 and the so-called 'Rose Revolution', when Saakashvili usurped the standing president Shevardnadze, former foreign minister of the Soviet Union under Mikhail Gorbachev. In attendance at the new president's inauguration were the US secretary of state, Colin Powell, and Russia's foreign minister, Igor Ivanov. Although Powell had been advising Saakashvili not to push Russia too far in the hope that the USA would come to his aid, Saakashvili raised the Georgian national flag to the EU anthem, *Ode to Joy*, and with a march past of Georgian troops American-style. In the documentary series, *Putin, Russia and the West* (BBC2, 2012), Powell recalled saying to himself, 'Oh boy! Igor's not going to enjoy this part of the performance!' To top it all off, the new president invited him in for talks at Tbilisi's City Hall, which was bedecked with rows of the Georgian flag and the Stars and Stripes.[8] Recalling his various encounters with Saakashvili up until the war, Powell summed up his assessment of the man:

> He was young and somewhat impulsive, and his impulses caused him to go further than he should, based on the situation he was in. We wanted to be supportive of him but I had to make it clear to him that, 'You might think this is in your vital interests [but] I'm not sure that it is. But it isn't in our national interest so don't get yourself into a situation that might overwhelm you and think that we might go racing in to rescue you. So be careful!'[9]

Saakashvili was depicted in media reports as a 'youthful, impetuous leader' (*Daily Telegraph*, 9 August 2008); and Georgia's 'best hope of furthering democracy in a poor neighbourhood. (His) Colombia Law School degree and fluent English mark him out from the many communist-era apparatchiks. But his detractors argue that the smooth facade masks a firebrand nationalist' ('Georgia's Moderniser: Mikheil Saakashvili', *Sunday Telegraph*, 10 August 2008). The *Observer* called him 'a man of contradictions': while he appeared 'remarkably Western and cautious', he sounded like 'a hard line nationalist'. Another article in the same issue – headlined, 'Georgia's Volatile Risk Taker has Gone Over the Brink' – described him 'veering between warmonger and peacemaker, democrat and autocrat' (10 August 2008). He was a 'bombastic loser [who] likes to be the centre of attention' (*Sunday Mirror*, 10 August 2008), a leader who was 'no more a convinced liberal than Vladimir Putin' (*Daily Telegraph*, 11 August 2008). The *Times* said he was 'no model democrat' and that he had been accused of 'verified cases of intimidation of his political opponents ... In taking advantage of the distraction of the Olympics, he looks sneaky, and so jeopardises his claim to the moral high ground' (11 August 2008).

The *Daily Mail* was generally sympathetic of Saakashvili and what he symbolised. He was, 'everything that Putin despises: fervently pro-Western, an ardent supporter of George Bush and an outspoken critic of Russian attempts to expand its sphere of influence' (12 August). But the paper still gave space to columnist Stephen Glover for a withering assessment of the Georgian leader. Glover concluded that Saakashvili 'may come across as an American-educated smoothie who talks the language of democracy, but he has behaved like a crude Caucasus warlord who lacks even the most elementary sense of statecraft' (*Daily Mail*, 11 August 2008). Three days later, he referred to 'the half-witted President Saakashvili ... a fool who has single-handedly undermined Western interests' (*Daily Mail*, 14 August 2008). In a column for the *Mail on Sunday* – 'Will Someone Send This Sabre-Rattling Twit a History Book?' – Peter Hitchens said that the Georgian leader 'was adept at bombastic propaganda' and that his 'opponents and critics fall victim to blatantly Soviet-style methods of intimidation' (17 August 2008).

A profile of the president in the *Independent* – 'High-stakes Gambler who Risked his Country and Links with the West' – described him as 'a loose cannon [with] a ruthless and impulsive streak [and who] in recent days has looked like a man who bit off more than he could chew' (12 August 2008). The *Guardian* online thought that he 'cuts a more sympathetic figure than the dour Vladimir Putin, the Russian prime minister, or his sidekick, the nondescript president Dmitry Medvedev'; but one of its contributors, James Poulos, described him as 'an imperfect leader, prone to beating his domestic opposition in the streets' (12 August 2008).

The overwhelming media impression of the Georgian leader, then, appeared to reflect the same ambivalence about his character that informed NATO's cautious approach to Georgia's push for membership. As to the reasons why he chose to send his army into South Ossetia, against the implicit advice of the US State Department, media reporting drew slightly different conclusions. One was the unqualified conclusion that Saakashvili exercised poor judgement and that the blame for the war lay with him; the other, rather qualified conclusion was that because of his character weaknesses, he fell for a Russian trap to draw him into a conflict he could never win, giving Russia the excuse it needed to annex South Ossetia and Abkhazia once and for all.

The invasion of South Ossetia was 'a gamble' (*Sunday Times*, 10 August 2008) taken by 'a man who has proved himself both one of the West's staunchest allies, and its greatest liability' (*Daily Mail*, 11 August 2008). For the *Independent*, the decision to go to war and provoke Russia raised 'serious questions about the judgement of President Saakashvili' (11 August 2008). The *Guardian* pointed out that many European governments are lukewarm about him, regarding [him] as 'his own worst enemy' (13 August 2008). Saakashvili, said a headline in the *Times*, 'Banked on Russia not having (the) will to fight' (9 August 2008), which was, the paper thought, a 'fundamental, disastrous miscalculation ... a disastrous misjudgement' (12 August 2008). Saakashvili 'recklessly miscalculated' (*Daily Mirror*, 12 August 2008) and his actions were drawing criticism as 'needlessly provocative' (*New York Times*, 12 August 2008). The *Daily Mirror* columnist Kevin Maguire put it most bluntly: 'attention-seeking Mikhail Saakashvili, triggered this conflict' ('Putin's Wrong ... But He Wasn't the Aggressor', 13 August 2008). And looking back after the French-brokered ceasefire, on 12 August 2008, the *Independent on Sunday* concluded that the brutal attack on South Ossetia's capital, Tskhinvali, 'stands out as the most disastrous mistake' of many that Saakashvili had made since the initial invasion (17 August 2008). From an American perspective, the *New York Times* explained that 'the Bush administration ... recognizes that Russia has legitimate security interests, and that Mr. Saakashvili has played a dangerous game of baiting the Russian bear' (*New York Times*, 9 August 2008).

The problem with the 'Russian Trap' theory was that there was scarcely any evidence presented for it in media reporting. Under the headline – 'The Suave New York Lawyer who Swallowed Putin's Bait' – the *Daily Telegraph* concluded that 'Saakashvili has handed Russia a victory it could scarcely have dreamed of' (9 August 2008). It then asked,

How did he make such a catastrophic blunder? The answer appears to lie in Mr Saakashvili's own character. While supporters praise him as a passionate and patriotic leader ... critics say he is bombastic, impulsive and confrontational and [that] his impetuosity triggered a crisis of Cold War proportions.

(*Daily Telegraph*, 9 August 2008)

The same formula applied in the *Times* ('How Georgia Fell into its Enemies' Trap', 9 August 2008); the *Independent on Sunday* ('Saakashvili ... may have stepped into a Russian trap', 10 August 2008); and the *Daily Mail* ('So Why did They Blunder into this Trap?', 11 August 2008). For the *Sun*, it was all down to Putin, 'a judo black belt skilled at using an opponent's momentum to his advantage' ('How Georgia Fell into Putin's Trap', 11 August 2008).

When it came to reporting and debating the West's response to the war in Georgia, the media were united in laying the blame on Russia and warning of its threat to Western interests, particularly control of the gas pipeline that runs through Georgia from Azerbaijan to Turkey. However, there was a significant difference of perspective when it came to how the West was handling the problem. The conservative press bemoaned the powerlessness of NATO and the EU, and contrasted that to what they saw as a much tougher response from the USA. The liberal press, on the other hand, were critical of the Western response in general, preferring to see it limited to symbolic action and empty rhetoric.

The West Responds

The *Daily Telegraph* commented that 'President George W. Bush was the only leader who publicly supported Georgia's position precisely because America feared that anything less would trigger Russian intervention. Sadly, his judgment has been vindicated' (9 August 2008). In his column for the same paper, 'The West must start to hit Russia where it hurts – in the roubles', Simon Heffer called for wide-sweeping economic sanctions against Russia, dismissed the relevance of NATO and concluded that, 'Only America has the muscle, the will and the sense of leadership to deal with this' (*Daily Telegraph*, 13 August 2008). A headline in the *Daily Mail* described Russia's invasion of Georgia and its aerial bombardment of major towns and cities, including the capital, Tbilisi, as a 'Blitz on Georgia' and was subtitled: 'This can't be Allowed in the 21st Century, Bush Protests' (12 August 2008). When the US president ordered 'humanitarian aid' flights into Georgia on 13 August 2008, the headlines on the next day described the move as a 'Georgia rescue' (*Sun*, 14 August 2008); a 'challenge' (*Daily Mail*) and 'a message' to Russia (*Independent*). The *Daily Mirror* saw it as 'a none-too subtle reminder of American military might' and in another item, headlined, 'U.S Gets Tough', it reported warnings to Russia 'to stop behaving like a Cold War bully over its conflict with Georgia ... [and] realise it could no longer push neighbours around as it had in the Soviet era' (14 August 2008).

The war in Georgia coincided in the USA with the presidential election campaign and became an issue of debate between the principal candidates: Democrat senator, Barack Obama and Republican senator, John McCain. In contrast to Obama's cautious approach to dealing with Russia, emphasising diplomacy over military intervention, McCain took a hard-line stance, advocating the isolation and punishment of Russia. Some conservative-leaning newspapers seemed to take this to be a serious proposition:

McCain plan to isolate and punish Russia (*Daily Telegraph*, 12 August)

McCain is man to tame Russia (*Sun*, 12 August)

If it's war we want, McCain will deliver (*Sunday Times*, 17 August)

A *New York Times* item, 'War Puts focus on McCain's Hard Line on Russia' (11 August 2008), explained that this was more than just an opportunistic campaign ploy against Obama. It had been an evolving part of his foreign policy formulation ever since he entered into politics. The article recalled some of McCain's previous statements such as his nomination in 2005 of Mikheil Saakashvili for the Nobel Peace Prize; and his call in 2006 for Russia to be expelled from the G8 (Group of 8 leading industrialised nations). More revealing than that, perhaps, was the revelation in this article that McCain's foreign policy adviser, Randy Schuenemann, had lobbied on behalf of the Georgian government up until March 2008.

In Britain, the right-wing media attacked the Labour governments' belated response to the Russian invasion. A *Daily Telegraph* editorial, 'Four days of silence that condemn Britain', welcomed a statement of condemnation from Prime Minister Gordon Brown but asked 'why had it taken four days since the crisis began for the British Prime Minister to comment in such terms? Where, too, has the Foreign Secretary [David Miliband] been?' (12 August 2008). The *Sun* noted the visit to Georgia on 16 August 2008 by David Cameron, the leader of the opposition, 'the first major British politician to visit the small, democratic country being systematically trashed by the mighty Russian bear.' While the paper doubted it would make any difference to the situation, it argued that 'at least the Tory leader is taking a strong stand against increasing Russian belligerence' (*Sun*, 16 August 2008). The most urgent question, it concluded was: 'Where on earth are Gordon Brown and his Foreign Secretary David Miliband?' (*Sun*, 16 August 2008). For the answer, the *Sun* might have checked back on its edition on 12 August 2008, where it reported that 'Gordon Brown blasted Russia yesterday and warned it risked creating a "humanitarian catastrophe".' In an article for the *Sunday Times*, 'We must make Moscow pay for this blow against democracy', David Cameron decided it was time to impose a stricter visa regime on Russian citizens who 'value their ties to Europe – their shopping and their luxury weekends … Russian armies can't march into other countries while Russian shoppers carry on marching into Selfridges' (17 August 2008).

There was also criticism of the divisions within NATO and, thus, its failure to decide a coherent policy for action in response to Russia's invasion of Georgia:

A divided West plays into Russia's hands (*Sunday Times*, 17 August)
Divided they stand: NATO searches for a strategy to confront Russia (*Times*, 19 August)
NATO is divided over policy on Russia (*Daily Telegraph*, 20 August)
Unity, not division, should be the model (*Guardian.com*, 20 August)

The *Sunday Times* (10 August 2008) and the *Daily Telegraph* (11 August 2008) cited a background briefing from the US State Department that there were 'few options' for dealing with Russia, not least military intervention. For the *Daily Mail*, the limited response from Washington served as '... a brutal reminder ... of the West's impotence in a region which contains key oil and gas pipelines, on which we depend' (11 August 2008). The *Guardian* acknowledged that the crisis 'exposed the west's lack of leverage over a resurgent Russia' and that, in 'the tussle for supremacy in a vital strategic region, the balance has tilted. Russia has successfully deployed its firepower in another country with impunity for the first time since communism's collapse' ('Georgian Conflict Leaves West Reeling and Russia Walking Tall', *Guardian.com*, 12 August 2008). In its edition on the next day, the newspaper said that the impotence of the West's response had been

laid bare before the world. The root causes of [its] alarming helplessness lie in the broad strategic failure of the Bush administration's foreign policy. It first alienated and then badly misread Putin's character and intentions, only realising his true threat to Western interests after it was too late.

(Guardian.com, 13 August 2008)

A *Daily Telegraph* editorial opened with the admission that: 'The West is in no position, practically or morally, to go to war with Russia' yet closed by saying that a resolution of the issue 'may yet come down to a face-off between Russia and America' (*Daily Telegraph*, 11 August 2008). The *Sun*'s political editor, Trevor Kavanagh, wrote that: 'The Russian Bear is not swayed by hand-wringing or threats' from the EU, which he described as 'a flabby alliance of mostly timid nations ... As France calls for a European army of chocolate soldiers from 27 bickering member states, Russia demonstrates in a flash how to use the iron fist' (*Sun*, 11 August 2008). In its editorial of 12 August 2008, 'Why brutal Putin doesn't fear the West', the *Daily Mail* complained that: 'The West wrings its hands. Appeasement, clumsiness, an absence of clear thinking and a woeful lack of unity have helped bring us to this sorry pass. We urgently need to do better.' In an article for the *Guardian* online, Alexandros Petersen, director of the think-tank, Caspian Policy Center, condemned the EU and NATO for 'either wringing their hands or sitting on them', while Russia bombed Georgia 'to finally smash the dream of a Europe whole and free.' ('The Kremlin is Flexing its Muscles at Feeble Europe', 12 August 2008).

The *Guardian* columnist, Simon Jenkins, said that the war in Georgia 'displayed the failure of the west's policy of belligerence towards Vladimir Putin's Russia' and exposed Western leaders as 'a bunch of tough-talking windbags' (13 August 2008). In the following week, he described NATO as 'useless' and, with reference to the alliance's operations in Afghanistan and Kosovo, 'a rotten fighting force … which in Kabul is on the brink of being side-lined by exasperated Americans. Nor is it any better at diplomacy: witness its ham-fisted handling of east Europe' (*Guardian*, 20 August 2008). The *Independent on Sunday* described the Western response as:

> waffle and, where it has not been meaningless guff, it has actually made matters worse … [If] Western leaders adapt their rhetoric to a more thoughtful realism – then it is possible that something positive might come out of the summer of 2008. But only if Western leaders show a clear-eyed understanding of Russia's fears and change the tone and substance of their response.
>
> ('Do not Feed the Bear's Paranoia',
> *Independent on Sunday*, 17 August 2008)

On the following day, its sister paper, the *Independent*, warned that 'the language of international diplomacy … is threatening to careen dangerously out of control, embracing one country after another and locking the United States and Russia into a dangerous cycle of retaliatory threats' (18 August 2008). In his column for the *Mail on Sunday*, Peter Hitchens asked:

> When will our political class stop trying to grow hairs on their teenage chests by starting wars and deploying forces we no longer have? Why should we get entangled in this? What business is it of ours if Russia wants friends and allies on its borders, rather

than a weird NATO alliance, kept on life support long after it triumphantly achieved its purpose. What is NATO for now? Does anybody know? If they know, will they say?

(*Mail on Sunday*, 17 August 2008)

The *Guardian* argued in its online edition that:

The west's response to the Georgian crisis should not be to re-erect fresh lines of confrontation through the middle of Ukraine, or along the Caucasus mountain range. It should not be to install 'pipeline police' guarding the oil pipeline from Baku. It should not be to establish major military bases along that new border.

('NATO Stops Here', *Guardian.com*, 14 August 2008)

Not only would that appear to Russia to be Western expansionism and encirclement, it would entrench 'the hawks in the Kremlin' and undermine the country's 'dwindling band of democrats.' Ultimately, it would be 'a recipe for war, which Europe has no will to fight' ('NATO Stops Here', *Guardian.com*, 14 August 2008).

However, there was an ideological and historical 'elephant in the room' here that these criticisms either refused or neglected to acknowledge: the West's own record of wars and 'humanitarian interventions' since the end of the Cold War, all of which had spurious legitimacy and death tolls that dwarfed even those of Russia's bloody conflicts in Chechnya. In a sample of over 490 newspapers items analysed for this case study, only one, by Stephen Glover in the *Daily Mail* (14 August 2008) highlighted the 'preposterously hypocritical' reaction of the USA and UK,

two governments [that] have made a speciality in recent years of invading other people's countries, using pretexts and justifications that sometimes seemed even less soundly based than Russia's in the case of Georgia … Let's cut out the moralising … In the mouths of leaders of governments which have waged bloody and often indefensible wars, it makes us sound like ineffectual hypocrites.

('Yes, This War is Wrong but after Iraq, the West's Moralising is an Outrage', *Daily Mail*, 14 August 2008)

This single item accounted for 1,102 words out of a total of 320,000 words for the total sample.

THE CRIMEAN CRISIS (2014)[10]

The crisis over Crimea emerged in February 2014 against the backdrop of political instability in Ukraine. Growing protests on the streets of the capital, Kiev, forced from office the Russian-friendly but corrupt president, Victor Yanukovych, which resulted in turn in the mass resignation of the government. The formation of a new, more nationalist and right-wing administration was viewed with suspicion and growing anxiety among the country's ethnic Russian minority, especially in the Crimea, a region that was originally part of Russia but 'gifted' to Ukraine in 1954, during the Soviet era. It was also viewed with some consternation in Moscow, whose interests in the Crimea were significant. The region's capital, Sevastopol, was the base for Russia's Black Sea fleet and a garrison of 25,000 troops. As tensions in the region mounted over the following weeks, with confrontations in the capital between pro-Russian and pro-Ukrainian demonstrators, Vladimir Putin appeared to lend tacit support for a return of the region to Russian jurisdiction by way of a referendum. On 2 March 2014, a small force of Russian troops, without military ID or insignia, entered the region and took control of its two principal airports, a development that turned the situation into an international crisis. However, it quickly became apparent that the response from the USA, Britain, NATO and the EU was going to be limited to threats of economic and diplomatic sanctions. On 16 March 2014, the people of Crimea voted in a referendum and returned a 95.5 per cent vote in favour of a return to Russian jurisdiction, a result received in the West with suspicion and derision. On 17 March 2014, a triumphant President Putin welcomed the result in parliament and moved immediately to sign it into law.

The media analysis that follows is based on a sample 612 newspaper items, published between 25 February–20 March 2014. It focuses principally on the portrayal of Putin and the Western response to his intervention and annexation of Crimea.

Putin

As with the Western media coverage of the Russian presidential elections, the Second Chechen War and the Russo–Georgian War, the principal, Western media response to the Crimean crisis was to personalise it as a problem with Vladimir Putin. However, there was a new, more extreme element to their image construction: a profile that ascribed to the Russian leader, without a shred of clinical evidence, symptoms typical of paranoia or even paranoid schizophrenia. This became the reference point for speculation about the implications of his psychological instability for East–West relations into the future.

The British press produced a picture of the Russian leader, Vladimir Putin, as a complex and unstable personality who posed a threat not just to the Ukraine but to 'world peace'. Among the elite newspapers, the most negative and subjective portrait by a long way was that of the *Guardian*, which characterised the Russian president throughout the crisis as a 'pugnacious', 'triumphant' but 'frustrated' leader with a 'nostalgia for Soviet times'; he was a cross between an 'unrepentant Cold War warrior' and a 'pre-1917 imperial nationalist'; a 'KGB professional' prone to 'zero-sum thinking', 'flights of apparent fancy', 'bombast', 'bile' and 'paranoia'. The 'irredentist adventure' in the Crimea was 'a carve up' and a 'land grab' by a man at the head of an 'expansionist', 'de facto dictatorship'. The *Guardian's* sister paper, the *Observer* (Sunday) described Putin as an 'unpleasant' and 'ruthless man' who demonstrated 'calm calculation' in his handling of the wider crisis in the Ukraine. For the *Daily Telegraph*, Putin was a 'steely', 'determined', 'strong man'; 'exerting power in the shadows' and advancing his cause in Crimea using 'a covert network of influence'; his 'paranoia' and 'macho politics', as well as his 'territorial aggression', explained the motivations for his 'land grab', or 'annexation', of the Crimean peninsula. Putin was described in the *Times* as 'Vlad the invader', 'chairman of the world's unofficial Autocrat's Club' and a 'master of the dark arts'; he was an 'aggressive' and 'enraged' politician in the pursuit of 'power games' and 'brinkmanship'. The *Sunday Times* described him as a man of 'ruthless clarity of purpose' and 'permanent rage', ready to promote his policies by way of 'bribery', 'bluff' and 'threat'. The *Daily Mail* saw him as a 'bogey man' and a 'puppet master' whose public demeanour was 'defiant', 'aggressive' and 'emotional'; it, too, described the return of Crimea to Russia as a 'land grab', an 'annexation' and, alluding to Hitler's annexation of Austria in 1938, a 'Russian anschluss'.[11] With the exception of the *Daily Mail* and *Mail on Sunday*, coverage in the popular press – the *Sun*, the *Daily Mirror* and the *Daily Star* – was minimal and produced little other than bad headline puns on the name of the Russian leader: for example, 'Vlad's Troops Go Russian In!' (*Sun*, 2 March 2014); 'The Vladfather' (*Sun*, 17 March 2014); and 'Putin Our Place' (*Daily Mirror*, 19 March 2014). The *Sun* depicted him as a 'tyrant' and 'classic Bond villain' engaged in a 'titanic game of bluff' in the Crimea, while the *Daily Mirror* referred to him as a 'hard man' and the new 'Rasputin'. Of all the British newspapers in the sample, the *Independent* was the most sober in its assessment of Putin, describing him as a 'confident', 'business-like', if somewhat 'prickly' leader in his dealings with the media. The paper's strongest characterisation of his actions was to describe them, at best, as empty 'sabre-rattling'; at worst, as post-Soviet 'revanchism'; its sister paper, the *Independent on Sunday*, depicted him as a man of 'calm calculation', if somewhat 'unpleasant' and 'ruthless' by nature.

The composite media portrait of Putin here does not amount to a psychological or clinical profile based on scientific method and evidence; although that did not stop the US-based website, *Psychology Today*, lending Putin's enemy image some spurious legitimacy. In a piece titled, 'The Danger that Lurks Inside Vladimir Putin's Brain', Professor Ian H. Robertson of Trinity College Dublin concluded that 'contempt is key to Putin's troubling psychological profile'. Posted on 17 March 2014, the day after the referendum, Robertson explained that Putin's contempt for international leaders, institutions and the rule of law is rooted in his 'Marxist-Leninist worldview', which treats such things as 'instruments of capitalist or bourgeois oppression'; and in a national or political culture 'where the ends justified the means.' Without clinical evidence, Robertson declared that 'there can be little doubt that [Putin's] brain has been neurologically or physically changed so much that he firmly and genuinely believes that without him, Russia is doomed'. In his closing section, sub-headed,

'How to handle a man like Putin', the professor offers a prognosis using language more akin to a neoconservative ideologue than a professional psychologist:

> *I have little doubt* that Putin feels personally humiliated by the fall of the Soviet Union and its empire and that, fuelled by power and with a blindness to risk, he will work ever harder to make good that humiliation through further dangerous adventures. He will be all the more driven by his feeling of personal and national superiority to the contemptibly weak, decadent and cowardly western powers – as he probably sees them.
>
> So how should the West respond? *Psychologically speaking*, the very worst response would be appeasement because this will simply fuel his contempt and strengthen the justification for his position. Strong consequences have to follow from his contempt for international law and treaties. This will cost the West dearly, economically speaking, but the longer-term costs of appeasement will make the costs of strong, early action appear trivial in retrospect.[12] [Emphasis added]

In past conflicts, such as the Gulf War in 1991 and the Iraq War in 2003, similar language to describe the Iraqi leader, Saddam Hussein, as a 'monster' and a 'new Hitler', functioned as the drumbeats of war, softening domestic publics for the 'inevitable' conflict to come (see, for example, Philo and McLaughlin, 1995; Miller, 2004; Tumber and Palmer, 2004). The caricature of Putin as a psychopath during the Crimea crisis, on the other hand, appeared to serve two different purposes. The first was to deflect from Western responsibility for helping to provoke the crisis in the first place; and the second, intentionally or by default, was to distract from Western impotence in the face of a military force they were not ready or willing to confront.

The West Responds

There were two dominant, headline responses to Russia's annexation of the Crimea, both of which echoed with media reactions to the

Second Chechen War and Russia's invasion of Georgia. We had the 'get tough' theme:

Cameron Joins Merkel in Expressing Anxiety and Warns that 'The World is Watching' (*Independent*, 2 March)

A Line Must be Drawn (*Daily Telegraph*, 5 March)

Allies Must Act Together to Keep Putin in Check (*Daily Telegraph*, 12 March)

Confront Putin with Troops, Obama Told (*Times*, 15 March)

Putin Needs to Hear a Four-Letter Word: NATO (*Times*, 19 March)

We Have to Stand Up to Russia – It's a Rogue State (*Guardian*, 18 March)

The West's eventual response to the crisis was a transatlantic attempt to exert pressure on Russia by applying economic sanctions while at the same time pushing for diplomatic dialogue to end the crisis:

Kremlin's intervention in Ukraine violates the post-war order, says German chancellor as world powers draw up targeted sanctions (*Daily Telegraph*, 13 March)

West Fires First Sanctions Shot and Warns of New Cold War (*Daily Telegraph*, 18 March)

EU and US Impose Sanctions on Russian and Ukrainian Officials (*Guardian*, 17 March)

France Warns Russia it Could Cancel Warships Deal (*Guardian*, 18 March)

Piling the Pressure on Putin. Western Leaders Redouble Diplomatic Efforts with Moscow to Find a Peaceful Solution to the Escalating Crisis in Crimea (*Independent*, 10 March)

However, there was scepticism among some sections of the media about the effectiveness of the approach:

Britain Shies Away from Sanctions Against Putin (*Daily Mail*, 4 March)

Britain is Reduced to Shaking its Weedy Fist. Despite Strong Protests Against Russia's Actions, We are now Bystanders on the World Stage (*Daily Telegraph*, 5 March)

Ukraine has Revealed the New World of Western Impotence: Behind the Self-Righteous Bluster, All Our Leaders can do to Punish Russia is Cancel Summits, School Places and Shopping Trips (*Guardian*, 5 March)

Such Empty Threats ... Bet Vlad's Quaking (*Sun*, 6 March)

Powerless over Putin (*Daily Mirror*, 7 March)

Western Moral Posturing over Vladimir (*Daily Mirror*, 7 March)

Bring on the Sanctions, Says Sneering Kremlin (*Times*, 18 March)

Slap on the Wrist Suggests Lack of Appetite for Tough Approach (*Guardian*, 18 March)

Sanctions Won't Scare the Bear (*Daily Mail*, 18 March)

Europe Appears to have a Severe Shortage of Both Sticks and Carrots (*Independent*, 19 March)

Putin Our Place (*Daily Mirror*, 19 March)

Some editorial content provided a measure of perspective and warned against Western over-reaction, not all of it exclusive to the liberal press. In the *Daily Mail*, for example, Stephen Glover questioned the double-think that lay at the heart of Western rhetoric. 'Aren't we guilty of hypocrisy?' he asked:

When Russia was too weak for its complaints to be taken seriously, Britain and America bombed its regional ally Serbia in 1999, and then confiscated the Serbian enclave of Kosovo (which, by the by, remains a basket case bankrolled by the West). Why was that right and moral, whereas the return of Crimea to Russia with the approval of most of its population is wicked? I suggest that when it suits us, we do what we think we can get away with, but that when the Russians act on the same principle, we accuse them of violating moral norms and international law.

('Yes, Putin is a Bully but Aren't We Guilty of Moral Hypocrisy on Crimea?' *Daily Mail*, 20 March 2014)

Three column pieces in particular appeared in the *Guardian*, offering critical counterpoint to the newspaper's negative news coverage. In a guest column headed, 'This is No Cold War II', the historian Tarik Cyril Amar argued that:

> talk of a return to the cold war [in the West] is wide of the mark. Putin is not aggressive because he feels unchallenged by a flabby west. Since the end of the Soviet Union, the EU and NATO have enlarged at the impressive clip of roughly one new member every two years.
>
> (*Guardian*, 1 March 2014)

On that basis, he argued, the ongoing crisis in Ukraine, encouraged by the West, was from Putin's point of view 'a massive political defeat'.

In separate articles, senior *Guardian* journalists, Jonathan Steele and Seumas Milne highlighted the hypocrisy at the heart of the West's response. With long experience in reporting on Russian affairs, Steele pointed readers to NATO's role in provoking the crisis in Ukraine and the Crimea:

> The fact that NATO insists on getting engaged reveals the elephant in the room: underlying the crisis in Crimea and Russia's fierce resistance to potential changes is *NATO's undisguised ambition to continue two decades of expansion* into what used to be called 'post-Soviet space'. At the back of Pentagon minds, no doubt, is *the dream that a US navy will one day replace the Russian Black Sea fleet in the Crimean ports.*
>
> ('Not Too Late for Wisdom', *Guardian*, 3 March 2014; emphasis added)

On 6 March 2014, Seumas Milne opened his *Guardian* column with the remark that: 'Diplomatic pronouncements are renowned for hypocrisy and double standards. But western denunciations of Russian intervention in Crimea have reached new depths of self-parody.' With a swipe at the rhetoric of US Secretary John Kerry and his loud insistence that countries like Russia cannot just invade other countries on 'a trumped up pretext', Milne commented:

> That the states which launched the greatest act of unprovoked aggression in modern history on a trumped-up pretext – against Iraq, in an illegal war now estimated to have killed 500,000, along with the invasion of Afghanistan, bloody regime change in Libya, and the killing of thousands in drone attacks on Pakistan, Yemen and Somalia, all without UN authorisation – should make such claims is beyond absurdity.
>
> ('The Clash in Crimea is the Fruit of Western Expansion', *Guardian*, 6 March 2014)

THE DOWNING OF MALAYSIA AIRLINES FLIGHT MH17

On 17 July that year, Malaysia Airlines flight MH17 was shot down by a ground-to-air missile as it flew over eastern Ukraine, killing all on board (283 passengers and 15 crew). Allegations that the missile was launched by pro-Russian militia using a Russian missile were denied at the time but confirmed by the air crash investigation report, published in October 2015. The death toll alone ensured it would be an international news story but its context, the conflict in eastern Ukraine, once again brought Vladimir Putin into focus. Amid the usual rumours and speculation about who carried out the attack, and about why the aircraft was targeted, the international media were quick to target the Russian leader as ultimately responsible. After all, the accusation went, he had been supporting and arming the pro-Russian militia in eastern Ukraine. A sample of headlines, 18–20 July 2014, recall the media response to the annexation of Crimea:

> Global Outrage Aimed at Russia (*Daily Telegraph*, 18 July)
> Putin in the Dock (*Times*, 19 July)
> World Rounds on Russia for Fomenting Violence (*Times*, 19 July)
> This Lying Brute who has to be Shackled (*Daily Mail*, 19 July)
> Blood on his Hands (*Sun*, 19 July)

Putin Must Choose: The Russian Leader is in the Dock (*Guardian*, 19 July)

The Fingers Point at Putin (*Independent*, 19 July)

Putin is Responsible for this Massacre. He Must Restrain his Dogs of War (*Independent*, 19 July)

Putin is a Pariah. He Must be Treated as Such (*Sunday Telegraph*, 20 July)

An Atrocity Waiting to Happen in Putin's Mad, Lying World (*Sunday Times*, 20 July)

Shame Putin (*Mail on Sunday*, 20 July)

It's Time Brutish Putin was Held to Account (*Observer*, 20 July)

Again, as with the Crimea crisis, the right-wing media demanded tough and coordinated international action against the Russian president, including the arming of Ukraine to defeat the Russian militia. This was based on the rhetoric emanating from hawkish US Republicans, including Senator John McCain and his 'hell to pay' threat, but with little consideration of the consequences in an already dangerous conflict (*Daily Telegraph* and *Daily Mail*, 18 July 2014). When it quickly became apparent that such a course was being ruled out in favour of more sanctions against Russia, they bemoaned Western weakness and division. This, of course, has been a major theme of Western media commentary ever since Putin came to power in 2000 and steered Russia out of the chaos of the post-Soviet era: that Putin is the strong man and the evil genius able to run rough shod over international order while the Western alliance stands by. However, in response to MH17, it was almost exclusively confined to the right-wing media.

For Dan Hodges in the *Daily Telegraph* (19 July 2014), the downing of MH17 and the lives lost '[marked] the death of British "soft power"' as defined by Tony Blair's concept of 'humanitarian interventionism'.

Britain and its American allies had attempted to reorder the world – most notably in Afghanistan and Iraq – and we had failed ... In the era of soft power, no one has any stature. The idea of the president of the United States influencing world affairs has now become as ludicrous as the idea of the British foreign secretary doing the same. The special relationship is now a mutual paralysis.

(*Daily Telegraph*, 19 July 2014)

Hodges closes by arguing that real power had shifted to Putin, his ally Assad in Syria and also to ISIS: 'And on that cold calculus, Britain is now a powerless nation' (*Daily Telegraph*, 19 July 2014). An article by Peter Foster in the same edition, played to the same theme. It was headlined, 'A New World Disorder. The West is paying the price for its complacency, weakness and lack of leadership', but the article was rather more specific about where the blame lay. '(The) shaky centre of Europe is holding', he began, but it was:

> hard not to hear the echoes of history in Europe's collective failure to confront naked Russian aggression. For weeks now, the US – supported by Britain, to the irritation of many of our European allies – has been demanding tougher sanctions against Moscow … But as so often in the past, a timid and divided European leadership demurred.
>
> (*Daily Telegraph*, 19 July 2014)

In the *Times*, Roger Boyes prefigured the populist rhetoric that was to emerge in the US about civilised world (us) versus 'barbarians' (them): 'Weak leadership from the White House has allowed Vladimir Putin to imagine himself strong', he argued.

> The fact is that we have stopped pushing Mr Putin on anything. This is a terrible policy that highlights a straightforward truth: that the East–West relationship is being mismanaged by the weak leader of a strong West and the apparently strong leader of a weak East. It is a recipe for mishap and impotence and explains why relations are worse now than at any time since the hottest years of the Cold War.
>
> (*Times*, 19 July 2014)

An editorial in the *Daily Mail* spoke of 'a conflict of polar opposites' in which 'Putin … the ruthless former KGB officer, focused with deadly intent on rebuilding the Soviet empire' stood against 'the frivolous, dithering politicians of the West. Looking for 'statesmen of stature to lead us through these deeply worrying times', it advised readers to discount an 'increasingly isolationist' USA and the EU. 'For too long', it complained, 'Western politicians have lived in a fools' paradise, deluding themselves that history stopped when the Berlin Wall fell … they must wake up and join the real world before it's too late' (19 July 2014).

There was little of this agonising in the liberal press, an exception being an article in the *Daily Mirror* by former Moscow correspondent, Angus Roxburgh. Writing under the headline, 'Why Putin Could Not Care Less What the West Thinks', he opens:

> Western leaders have always found Putin tricky to deal with. Now they find him impossible. He's the strongest leader Russia has had since Stalin and no one is going to push him around. Sometimes it looks as if Western leaders are running scared.
>
> (*Daily Mirror*, 19 July 2014)

The article ends with the old familiar theme – the powerless West in face of Putin's contempt: 'There is little the West can do. In fact, the more we criticise him, the more popular he gets at home' (*Daily Mirror*, 19 July 2014).

As shown so far, the Western media construction of Russian military interventions has been marked by a clearly defined enemy image of Putin and Russia. It is an image which is completely consistent with that seen in the reporting of Vladimir Putin's ascendancy to power at home since the year 2000. It was underscored by a narrative of an impotent, divided West, struggling to respond decisively to its resurgent old enemy. However, the final case study to follow, the reporting of Russia's intervention in the Syrian War, in 2015, was to offer up an apparent anomaly. Unlike with Chechnya, Georgia and Ukraine/Crimea, the West was not in position to issue condemnation or call for immediate withdrawal because since 2014 a US-led coalition had entered the war in support of the Syrian opposition forces. This was the first time since Russia's intervention of Afghanistan in 1979 that it was to find itself in opposition to US-backed forces, a situation with potentially dangerous consequences for the Middle East, and globally.

RUSSIAN INTERVENTION IN SYRIAN CIVIL WAR IN 2015

Russia entered into the complex and bloody war in Syria on 30 September 2015 at the behest of its long-time ally. Although its ostensible objective was to target Islamic State in Iraq and the Levant (ISIL) and allied Islamic groups such as al-Nusra Front,[13] its real priority was clear. This was to provide mainly aerial support to Syrian state forces, along with their allies from Iran and the Lebanon (Hezbollah), in the battle with domestic opposition militias such as the Syrian Free Army. This section will examine media responses to three key moments: the initial intervention, the partial withdrawal of Russian forces announced on 14 March 2016, and the involvement of the remaining contingent in the recapture of the city of Aleppo in November and December that year.

What stands out in the media reporting of the intervention is a shift in the tone of the content. First, there was the near absence of the pejoratives to describe Vladimir Putin that so marked newspaper reporting and debates about him compared to the coverage of the wars in Chechnya and Georgia, and the annexation of Crimea. Indeed out of a total of 220 items covering the three key moments mentioned above, only three came close. The *Times* referred mockingly to a nickname given to the Russian president by Assad's supporters who, of course, welcomed his intervention: 'Abu Ali Putin' (11 October 2015). During the bombing of Aleppo in November–December 2016, the *New York Times* featured an article by academic Stephen Sestanovich headed, 'The Two Putin Problem' (25 November 2016). It was in effect a warning to President-elect, Donald Trump, that there were two sides to his Russian counterpart that he had to be careful about: 'one confident, cagey and effective; the other defensive, isolated and unsure of himself (with) a reputation for dishonesty and double-dealing' (*New York Times*, 25 November 2016). And as Russia helped recapture Aleppo from opposition groups, a *Daily Mirror* editorial condemned Putin and called for the West to 'Face Up to This Bully', who it also described as a 'cocksure strongman' and an 'autocrat' (24 December 2016).

However, this scaling down of the hostile pejoratives in the Western media did not mean an absence of analysis about the implications of Russia's intervention in Syria for its relationship with the West. There was plenty of that but it was framed within a different paradigm: more akin to that of the old 'Great Powers' rivalry of the nineteenth century. The prevalent media theme here was Vladimir Putin's penchant for bold tactical decisions, such as the partial withdrawal of Russian forces from Syria in March 2016, that would catch the West off guard:

Putin Keeps West Guessing with Shock Withdrawal from Syria
(*Times*, 15 March 2016)

President Vladimir V. Putin's typically theatrical order ... seemingly caught Washington, Damascus and everybody in between off guard – just the way the Russian leader likes it. By all accounts, Mr. Putin delights at creating surprises, reinforcing Russia's newfound image as a sovereign, global heavyweight and keeping him at the center of world events.
(*New York Times*, 15 March 2016)

Vladimir Putin has again demonstrated his capacity to surprise by announcing a withdrawal of Russian forces from Syria ... He caught everyone off-guard in the West and probably in Damascus, too ... This contrasts starkly with the lack of resolve in Washington and the capitals of the EU, which gave the Russian leader the opportunity to fill the vacuum.
(*Daily Telegraph*, 16 March 2016)

It looked, yet again, as if Washington had been caught out by Russia's president in a crisis which has repeatedly tested US credibility. [...] He believes – not without good evidence – that he can win credit with Russian public opinion whenever he appears to outfox the US.

(*Guardian*, 16 March 2016)

Putin, so the narrative went, was 'bringing Russia back to center stage as a global power' (*New York Times*, 14 March 2016). He was 'eager for Russia to be treated as an equal partner by global powers' (*Independent*, 15 March 2016). His 'game' was 'to neuter and divide the west – and he is succeeding. Russia wants to make us weak and, thanks to politicians in the USA and Europe, it is getting its way' (*Daily Telegraph*, 13 December 2015). The *Sunday Telegraph* columnist, Janet Daley, argued that:

> What drives Russia now ... is the naked desire to reassert its control over areas of the world where national pride dictates that it must not be eclipsed. Vladimir Putin may be presiding over a dying population and a failing economy, but if he can annex the Crimea and intimidate former satellite states in Eastern Europe without fear of NATO reprisal, as well as maintain the hideous Assad regime (with the help of his allies in Iran), then he is on top of the world.
>
> (*Sunday Telegraph*, 18 December 2016)

A variant of the theme was Putin's urge to outdo the USA. In response to Russia's partial withdrawal from Syria, in March 2016, Roger Boyes wrote that:

> The Russian president imagines that he can bamboozle the Obama administration in its final months. He did it before in 2013 when he averted a US attack on Assad and instead ordered the dictator to surrender his chemical weapons stocks. It was a brilliant tactical move, wrecking US credibility in the Middle East and contributing to Assad's survival.
>
> (*Times*, 16 March 2016)

And as Russia succeeded in helping Assad recapture Aleppo from opposition forces, the *Observer* explained that 'Russia's goals have been less about ideology, and more about realpolitik. Vladimir Putin now has a renewed stake in the region, at the expense of the US' (18 December 2016). An end-of-year review in the *Guardian* (31 December 2016) was headlined, 'Why Russia is now calling the shots in the Middle East. In the case of the Syria peace drive, Moscow is at the centre of decision making. The US, by contrast, ends 2016 out in the cold' (29 December 2016). For the *New York Times*,

> Mr. Putin has effectively marginalized the United States and maneuvered into position as the dominant international player in Syria. [...] At the moment, Mr. Putin looks like a master tactician for reasserting Russian influence in Syria, a client during the Cold War of the Soviet Union and more recently of Iran.
>
> (*New York Times*, 31 December 2016)

CONCLUDING REMARKS

This media narrative of the strong, decisive and powerful Putin versus an impotent, divided West is consistent with the reporting of successive presidential elections in Russia and it is consistent with the coverage of Chechnya, Georgia and Crimea. In all this media content, there was an absence of critical reflection on the West's decades-long push against Russia's 'near abroad', its regional sphere of influence and its buffer against foreign encirclement. Amid this discursive absence, the following extract from an article in the *New York Times*, by the former US ambassador to Russia, Michael A. McFaul,[14] could be read without a scintilla of irony:

> Mr. Putin is adept at short-term tactical responses to setbacks, but less talented at long-term strategy. Even with no response from the West, Mr. Putin's foreign adventures will finally fail, especially as domestic economic problems continue to fester. But the United States and its allies should seek to shorten that time by pushing back against Russia on multiple fronts. As Mr. Putin goes all in to

prop up his ally in Syria, we should do the same with our partners and allies – not only in Syria, but in Europe and around the world. … We must continue to pursue long-term foreign policy objectives that demonstrate American leadership and underscore Russia's isolation.

('The Myth of Putin's Strategic Genius',
New York Times, 23 October 2015)

This chapter has looked at media coverage of four of 'Putin's foreign adventures' with reference to analyses of the West's response to each and to how these were refracted through the prism of the enemy image which the media have played a major role in constructing. What is striking is the level of consistency there was within and between the four case studies and over the two decades of Vladimir Putin's ascendency. The coverage of Russia's involvement in the Syrian Civil War, however, throws up something of an anomaly, and that is an apparent 'softening' of Putin's image and a relative absence of Cold War rhetoric. This does not mean that media coverage was no less critical of Russia's role in Syria in support of Assad. Interviewed for this book, Mary Dejevsky argues that:

coverage has only become slightly less hostile towards Russia since it was clear the US and UK had basically lost – though it is still very negative, and totally lacks awareness of what Russia said it was trying to do: prevent a new Iraq/Libya in Syria, with total war and anarchy.[15]

6

Talking to Vladimir:
'Bigger, Tougher, Stronger, Meaner'

The US–Soviet summit was a perennial feature of Cold War diplomacy, among the most famous being the Yalta conference in 1945, in which the allied powers, including the Soviet Union under Joseph Stalin, discussed the outlines of a post-war, world order; and the Moscow Summit in 1988, in which Secretary General, Mikhail Gorbachev, welcomed Ronald Reagan, the first US president to visit the USSR in an official capacity. Summit meetings like these are usually organised and staged to deliver pre-agreed treaties on arms reduction, for example, but they are reported by the international media as much for their ritual and symbolism; and for what the personal relationship between presidents says about the diplomatic relationship between superpowers (Hallin and Mancini, 1989; McLaughlin, 2002). A look back at these summits in Europe reveals a ritual pattern. The US president takes the opportunity to meet with European allies, perhaps also attend a NATO summit. He presents a keynote speech, emphasising how the Atlantic alliance is underpinned by the values of freedom, democracy and security, and challenging the Soviet Union, now just Russia, to embrace those values, too. The summits themselves may include the signing of pre-agreed treaties on arms control and then finish with media conferences with the two leaders, whether individually or jointly. What this chapter seeks to show is how Vladimir Putin's summit meetings with US presidents Clinton, Bush and Obama largely conformed to this pattern; and how his first two summits with President Donald Trump appeared to mark a radical break from not just the pattern but with how they were reported.

CLINTON

Putin first met Clinton in Oslo in August 1999, just as he became Russian prime minister and had ordered the invasion of Chechnya. This was a brief, getting-to-know-you encounter during which the American president chided him about the invasion, describing it as 'an over-reaction'. However, the two leaders were to have just one formal summit; this was in Moscow, 4–5 June 2000, when Putin was beginning his first full term as president and Clinton was in his last few months of his second term. The meeting was set to formalise a Russian–American agreement to destroy between them 68 tonnes of weapons-grade plutonium and to continue dialogue around unresolved issues, chief among which was America's plan to roll out a Nuclear Missile Defense system (NMD), nicknamed 'son of Star Wars', to be based in Alaska and Europe. This and the expansion of NATO eastwards represented for Russia an existential threat and were also disputed among America's European allies in NATO. Germany and France in particular worry that admitting more East European countries, Ukraine and Georgia especially, might threaten trade links with Russia. And they are anxious about the NMD system not just because of its perceived threat to Russia but also because of its implication that, in the event of a nuclear war, Europe would become the principal battleground.

The Personal Dynamics

A key theme that helped to define coverage of the summit was the apparent differences between the leaders in terms of personality and political power. Before the event even began, Putin proposed that the USA and Russia work together to create a joint missile defence system against threats from 'rogue states' such as North Korea and Iran. This was reported by the *Times* as 'a bold challenge' from Putin to an American president 'hamstrung by his lame duck status' (3 June 1999) and his 'sleekest bit of footwork' in the negotiations (5 June 1999). The *Independent on Sunday* (4 June 1999) called it 'a deft piece of pre-summit manoeuvring', putting his opposite number in 'a tricky position' before talks began and showing that he would 'provide a more complex and more formidable challenge to the USA than his predecessor, Boris Yeltsin', with whom he had struck up a very friendly relationship. A headline in the *Times* (5 June 1999), 'No Hugs or Sax Solos as Bill and Vlad Play Hard to Get', alluded to summit evenings when Clinton would entertain Yeltsin with his saxophone playing. With Putin, however, 'It was never going to be like old times. Instead of the bear-like soulmate [Yeltsin] he spent the weekend with a judo black-belt who has a handshake like a karate chop.' The *Express* (5 June 1999) summed the meeting up with the headline, 'Clinton Cuts No Ice with Frosty Putin'. The *Independent* (3 June 1999) asked, 'Can we trust Putin, or is he another Stalin?', and concluded that:

> the best that can be said of Mr Putin is that his apparent lack of character – he appears to have the moral backbone of an earthworm – is an indirect reflection of the fact that Russia is no longer a country of undiluted chaos. For all the talk of Stalinism [he] seems better suited to being a technocrat than a dictator.
>
> (*Independent*, 3 June 1999)

The *New York Times* (5 June 1999) and the *Guardian* (6 June 1999) quoted the judgement of an unnamed US 'official' at the summit, that the Russian leader was 'a cold fish' and a 'control freak' but that on serious issues such as arms control those qualities 'might not be bad'.

The Talks

Clinton's tour of Europe should have been a propaganda opportunity to emphasise NATO unity and American leadership, and to set the agenda of the forthcoming meeting with the Russian leader. Instead, his efforts to promote the virtues of an NMD system exposed serious disagreement within NATO allies. This was ignored by the right-wing media, with only the liberal *Guardian* and the *Independent* referring to the fractures in their coverage. While they reported 'blunt public criticism' and 'rising anger' in Germany (*Guardian*) and Clinton's failure to sell the system to his allies (*Independent*), the right-wing press framed it solely as a dispute between the US and

Russia. On 5 June 1999, the second day of the summit, the *Times* defined the NMD system as a 'bone of contention' and the 'chief obstacle to an arms control breakthrough'. The *Express* reported that Clinton and Putin 'could not resolve the crucial dispute over American plans for a Star Wars missile defence shield, protecting the US and its European allies from nuclear strikes by rogue states like Iraq and North Korea' (5 June 1999). The *New York Times* said that the two leaders ended the summit with mutual praise 'but without narrowing the differences over the national missile defense system', and that Clinton had failed in one of his key summit aims, to ease Russian 'anxieties' about and 'soften Kremlin resistance' to the plan (5 June 1999).

BUSH

There is an anecdote about Vladimir Putin and his summit meeting with US President George W. Bush, in Moscow, May 2002. He introduced Bush to his black labrador, Konni, telling him that Konni was 'bigger, tougher, stronger, faster and meaner' than Barney, the US president's Scottish terrier. Bush took it with a smile – it would have been ridiculous to argue about it – but it seemed to be another Putin power play. In this early phase of his relationship with the American president, was Putin reinforcing the message to Bush and/or his domestic audience that he was 'Top Dog'? Or was it just a joke? He met with George W. Bush several times during the US president's two terms of office, 2000–2008. This section will sample coverage of three of those: an introductory meeting in Ljubjana, Slovenia, 16 June 2000; an impromptu summit at the summer home in Maine of Bush's father and ex-president, George Bush, Snr, 2–3 July 2007; and a farewell meeting in the Russian resort of Sochi, 6 April 2008, as Bush approached the end of his second term and as Putin was to give way to the newly elected President of Russia, Dmitry Medvedev.

The Personal Dynamics

Before his first meeting with Putin in 2001, Bush had to negotiate a difficult first tour of Europe, starting on 12 June with a state visit to

Spain and taking in summit meetings of NATO in Brussels (13 June 2001) and the EU in Gothenberg (14–15 June 2001). The USA was facing public protests in Europe against its lukewarm commitment to ratifying the Kyoto Protocol (1997) on global warming, as well as NATO objections to its NMD system and its proposals for the expansion of the alliance eastwards to Russia's borders. Undeterred, the new president used a policy speech in Warsaw, on 15 June 2001, to emphasise his vision of NATO expansion. The media responded with headlines that were bound to be taken as a clear message to President Putin in advance of the summit:

> Bush Appeals for West to Expand Towards Baltic (*Daily Telegra*ph)
> NATO will Not Accept Putin Veto, Bush Says (*Times*)
> Bush Unveils Vision to push NATO Eastwards (*Daily Mail*)
> Bush: East Joins West (*Sun*)
> Bush Projects NATO to Russian Border ... Whether Russia Likes That or Not (*Guardian*)

Although Bush attempted to offset this rather aggressive pre-summit agenda with noises about Russia having nothing to fear from the advance of 'freedom loving peoples' to its borders and being an ally of the West against 'rogue states', his first meeting with Vladimir Putin seemed set for confrontation. The initial, personal dynamic between the two leaders would, then, provide clues for the media as to how the meeting would work out. So it was perhaps a surprise to Western publics to read headlines such as: 'Bush Finds a Friend in Putin After Euro Rows' (*Sunday Times*); 'Putin Warms to the Texan Cowboy' (*Sunday Express*); 'Superpower Thaw ... an Unexpectedly Warm Meeting' and 'Bush and Putin Make Friends in Slovenia' (*Independent on Sunday*). Or read reports that the two leaders had established 'warm personal relations' and 'a personal rapport' (*Sunday Telegraph*); that they had 'emerged from their first summit in jovial form' (*Sunday Times*); that they had struck 'a cordial personal relationship' (*Observer*); that they were 'putting their new friendship on a high plane of newfound trust' (*New York Times*); and that their 'handshakes and chuckles [signalled] a personal chemistry' (*Times*, 18 June 2001).

The Talks

The two-day summit in Ljubljana was to be dominated again by NMD and NATO expansion. As with the coverage of the Putin–Clinton meeting, in the previous year, there were two opposing media frames. The conservative press reported the differences but without explaining the reasons behind Russia's opposition. On NATO expansion, the *Daily Telegraph* noted that, 'Russia can only be alarmed by Mr Bush's implicit call for NATO to admit the Baltic states: Lithuania, Latvia and Estonia' (16 June 2001). The liberal *Independent*, by contrast, revealed the Russian objections to be somewhat more nuanced:

> Today's militarily diminished Russia might be able to stomach the entry of Slovenia and Slovakia ... even of other aspirants like Bulgaria and Romania. But it has made clear that NATO membership for one or all of the three Baltic countries, which from 1940 to 1991 were part of the Soviet Union itself, would be totally unacceptable. The entry of Lithuania, for instance, would place NATO astride the corridor linking Russia proper with its strategic Baltic coast enclave of Kaliningrad.
>
> (*Independent*, 16 June 2001)

On NMD, the *Sunday Telegraph* reported 'sharp differences between the two leaders', quoting a warning from Putin that the problem 'could only make American–Russian relations "more complicated"' (17 June 2001). But NMD was more than just a point of difference between the USA and Russia. Looking ahead to the summit, the *Guardian* described it as 'the home straight of Mr Bush's race to persuade sceptical European allies and hostile Russians of the need for ambitious missile defences to replace the security measures of the cold war' (16 June 2001). The *Observer* pointed out, a plan that 'many in Europe, Russia, and Washington fear would make the world a much more dangerous place' (17 June 2001). Indeed, the *New York*

Times revealed just how dangerous when it reported a warning from Putin after the summit that:

> if the United States proceeded on its own to construct a missile defense shield over its territory and that of its allies, Russia would eventually upgrade its strategic nuclear arsenal with multiple warheads – reversing an achievement of arms control in recent decades – to ensure that it would be able to overwhelm such a shield.
>
> (*New York Times*, 19 June 2001)

Seven years later, in 2008, Bush's push for an NMD was becoming more urgent as the USA had identified Poland and the Czech Republic as likely sites for installations. In a bid to assuage Putin's growing anger about the threat this posed, Bush invited the Russian president to an ad hoc summit at the genteel, well-heeled fishing village and seaside resort of Kennebunkport in the state of Maine, USA. Usually, George W. Bush preferred to host his domestic diplomatic meetings at his ranch in Texas but this was the location of his father's holiday home and his presence, with his diplomatic experience, might help smooth the way towards a resolution of these long-running disputes. Previews of what the American media called 'The Lobster Summit' were largely pessimistic about its chances of success. The *Daily Telegraph* remarked on 'a relationship that has soured since those heady early days' and, that on his departure from Moscow for the summit, 'a measured Mr Putin made clear he would not be swayed by the carefully-arranged atmospherics' (2 July 2007). The *Sunday Times* predicted that the summit was 'expected to be marred by sharp disagreements', particularly over NMD and reported that 'relations between Russia and America are approaching a post-cold-war freezing point' (3 July 2007).

The *Times* also referred back to the 'cordial and excited' meetings of that period, and how much the relationship had deteriorated since then: 'Now, after six months of Putin's sour accusations about US imperialism, and shrill threats to point Russian missiles at Europe, it is chilly' (3 July 2007). Yet these 'shrill threats' related to a not unreasonable objection from Russia that it would have to target missiles at Poland and the Czech Republic, if they agreed to admit US NMD sites – ballistic missile interceptors and radar installations respectively. American assurances that the system was designed to thwart attacks on the USA and Europe from 'rogue states' such as Iran and North Korea had always been viewed with studied scepticism by Moscow. The article conceded that Vladimir Putin had 'one good point: his complaint about the younger Bush's disregard for arms control treaties', without going further to explain how and why (*Times*, 3 July 2007). The crucial problem with NMD was that it undermined the defence assumptions behind successive treaties to limit the location and numbers of ballistic or strategic missiles. Under the Anti-Ballistic Missile Treaty of 1972, a US–Soviet pact, the siting of a national missile defence system outside the national territory was prohibited. When the USA withdrew unilaterally from the Treaty in 2002 to get around the ban and push ahead with developing NMD, Russia continued to observe it because, as the academic Vladimir Rukavishnikov (2008) notes, 'The ABM Treaty was critical to Russia as a confirmation of its status in the international arena, despite the loss of superpower status following the collapse of the Soviet Union.' As Chapters 3 and 4 of this book have noted, Russian national pride and the need to be taken seriously on the world stage are fundamental definers of Putin's psyche but ones that Bush or, for that matter the international media, never seemed to recognise or understand.

In the end, the headlines on the close of the summit, 3 July 2007, signalled a thawing out in the personal relationship between the presidents but overall failure to resolve the substantive issues:

Bush and Putin in Shield Standoff (*Daily Mail*)
Bush–Putin Talks Fail to Address Big Issues (*Guardian*)
Warmth, but Little Progress at Summit (*Independent*)
No Major Breakthroughs (*New York Times*)

The final, official meeting between the two men, in Sochi, 6 April 2008, came just as Putin was to hand over office to the newly elected president Dmitry Medvedev. It was, then, more of a farewell to Bush and an introduction to his successor than a major US–Russia summit but there was still some talking around the familiar points of dispute: NMD and NATO expansion eastwards to Russia's borders, as well as a new disagreement about independence for Kosovo. Some media headlines and reporting on the day after the meeting preferred to focus on signs of improving personal relations and extrapolating from them hope for future agreement between successor presidents:

Bush and Putin Edge Towards Missile Shield Breakthrough (*Times*)

Vlad to See Ya! … Perhaps They are Putin their Differences Aside (*Sun*)

Warm Words to End Summit as Leaders Vow to Heal Divisions (*Independent*)

'War Horses' Differ but see Hope for Future Accord (*New York Times*)

The *Daily Telegraph* and the *Guardian*, on the other hand, emphasised Bush's failure to get an agreement on NMD. The *Telegraph*'s report on proceedings was headlined, 'Bush goes home empty-handed as final summit ends in failure', and noted how NMD had come to define the Bush–Putin relationship and, more recently, 'an issue that has played a leading role in the alarming deterioration of East–West relations over the past year' (7 April 2008). The *Guardian* offered a much blunter assessment:

Vladimir Putin seems to enjoy his meetings with George Bush. Little wonder. The canny Russian president invariably runs rings around his American counterpart, starting with their first encounter in 2001 when he somehow convinced Bush they were soul mates. Yesterday's Black Sea summit was no exception. A great deal of backslapping, verbal pleasantries and even a spot of spontaneous after-dinner folk dancing (by the ever ingenuous Bush) could not disguise the fact the Russian leader had once again slammed the door in his visitor's face. More than anything, Bush wanted a deal on missile defence. It was his last chance to get it. It was what he had come for. And Putin sent him away empty-handed.

(*Guardian*, 7 April 2008)

A guest column or op-ed in the *New York Times* (7 April 2008) by James Carroll, of the *Boston Globe*, questioned the characterisation of Russia as unreasonable, even paranoid, in the face of Western defence policy. Headlined, 'Paranoia Backed by Just Cause', it is worth quoting at length here because it is a rare example in the media of a genuine critique of the fundamental assumptions of Western, anti-Russian propaganda:

When the United States pushes a missile defense system on Europe, locating critical elements in Poland and the Czech Republic, Moscow refuses to believe that Iran is the target. Russian complaints are dismissed as unfounded. When NATO expansion continues not only to Russia's border, but – if the Bush administration gets its way – into integral states of the former Soviet Union, Moscow's warnings of a new Cold War are taken to be slightly crazy … incoming president Dmitri Medvedev as well as outgoing leader Vladimir Putin, are labeled as paranoid … [It] seemed a long time since that 2001 encounter when, as President George W. Bush put it, he glimpsed 'a sense' of Putin's soul and liked what he saw. Now Putin's soul is stained with suspicion. Why does the man act as if nothing comes from the West but military threat? Might it be because, at the end of the Cold War, the non-violent dissolution of the Warsaw Pact was matched by a beefing up of its counterpart, the Atlantic alliance? Instead of dismantling a military juggernaut defined by enmity with Moscow, Washington flexed it like a muscle, as if Moscow were still an enemy … Without drawing a moral equivalence between Stalinist communism and American-style capitalism, there can be no excuse today for repeating a pattern that guarantees a Russian move from vulnerability to belligerence. When one side in a nuclear armed contest is paranoid, the other side is, too. Madness is mutual, even when leaders seem sane. Sane? Never mind Moscow. Who would apply the word sanity for what has come lately from Washington?

(*New York Times*, 7 April 2008)

OBAMA

The election in November 2008 of Barack Obama as the 44th US president was celebrated around the world as an historic moment in American history. Here was the first black candidate to stand for and win the highest office in the land, a Democrat who campaigned with high rhetoric about a new era in America of hope and confidence. 'Yes we can!', was his winning slogan in the call-and-response style of Black Gospel. But as he would find out in the domestic and international policy arenas, over two terms in office, the response was just as likely to be 'No you can't!', and this was no more true than in US–Russian relations. This section samples media coverage of two meetings: a leaders' summit in Moscow, in 2009, with Dmitry Medvedev as Russian president; and Obama's final meeting with Vladimir Putin at the G20 summit in Beijing, China, in 2015.

High on the agenda for the leaders' summit in Moscow were the two perennial issues: NATO expansion, in particular the sensitive question of Georgia's right to membership; and NMD, which threatened to get in the way of a major agreement on nuclear disarmament. The USA also wanted to get Russia to pressurise Iran to abandon its plans to achieve nuclear weapons capability. The Obama administration billed it as the 'Reset Summit', an attempt to repair deteriorating relations between the USA and Russia. US Secretary of State, Hillary Clinton, and Vice-President, Joe Biden, even presented to the Russian foreign minister a plastic switch with what they thought was the Russian word for reset. They were quickly corrected: the word they used meant, 'overload'.

Personal Dynamics

Although the event was officially billed as a getting-to-know-you meeting between presidents Obama and Medvedev, Prime Minister Putin was always present whether in person or as the metaphorical 'elephant in the room'. Watching the two men interact, the *Times* observed that:

> the bluff bonhomie between Mr Bush and Mr Putin [has been] replaced by a brisk business like mood between Mr Obama and Mr Medvedev, befitting their shared past as lawyers. There were no jokes or attempts to personalise the relationship – instead simply declarations of agreement and of differences.
>
> (*Times*, 7 July 2009)

The *Guardian* got:

> little sense from yesterday's summit that the two sides had managed to overcome the hostility and suspicion that character-ised relations between George Bush and Vladimir Putin. Nor was there much of the sparkle that has accompanied previous summits between US and Russian leaders.
>
> (*Guardian*, 7 July 2009)

As shown in Chapter 3, media coverage of the 2008 presidential election framed the election of Medvedev and the appointment of Putin as prime minister as a political ruse, allowing Putin to maintain power while still observing the constitutional niceties. The theme came into play again in reporting the Moscow Summit. The *Daily Telegraph* described Medvedev's attempt to conduct proceedings on an equal footing with his more powerful US counterpart as 'vainglo-rious' (7 July 2009). Not only did it not reflect the reality of Russia's loss of status since the end of the Cold War but it came from 'a man who is not even master of his own house. Few doubt that Russia's most powerful politician is Mr Medvedev's old boss: Vladimir Putin' (*Daily Telegraph*, 7 July 2009). As by way of evidence, the paper reported on the next day that, after a breakfast meeting with Obama, Putin left the summit proceedings for, 'a visit to a Hell's Angels-style motorcycle club called the Night Wolves, where he boasted of his recent wheelies. Russian television gave it almost as much coverage as Mr Obama's speech' (*Daily Telegraph*, 8 July 2009). However, the question of who was really in charge in Russia was most pronounced in the liberal press. The *Independent* reminded readers on each day of its coverage, 6–8 July 2009, that 'real power in the Kremlin remains very much in the hands of the Prime Minister, Vladimir Putin' (6 July), that Putin was 'still seen as the country's most powerful man' (7 July) and 'still the most powerful man in the country' (8 July). For the *Guardian*, Putin was 'the man whom most people regard as Russia's real ruler' (7 July 2009). And in the USA, the *New York Times* declared him to be 'the paramount political force in Russia' and reported that Obama started the summit by referring to 'President Putin' before quickly correcting himself (6 July 2009).

This embarrassing slip by the American president was nothing compared to his attempts to set the agenda for the summit. Before his arrival in Moscow, Obama told the media that he looked forward to meeting Medvedev, a 'man of the future' and dismissed Putin as a man with one foot in the past and the old way of doing things. The Russian prime minister responded by saying, 'We do not stand bow-legged! We are firmly standing on both our legs and always look to the future!' (InterFax, 7 July 2009). Then, in the course of the summit, President Obama warned Russia to stop interfering in neighbouring countries, respect Georgia's right to NATO membership, to get out of 'old ways of thinking' and stop viewing the USA as an enemy. Some observers suggested that such an aggressive stance was in fact a tactic to exploit an apparent split between Medvedev and Putin, a theory that both men dismissed as nonsense. In an editorial headlined, 'Pressing the Wrong Buttons', the *Guardian* berated the American approach, saying 'it is not for the US president to play Russian politics by seeking to exploit differences in tone between president and premier. The US has to deal with the Russian government, whoever leads it' (6 July 2009).

The Talks

The NMD system once again loomed large in summit talks between Obama and Medvedev, threatening to impede progress towards a framework agreement on further nuclear arms reduction. President Medvedev was determined to use the framework agreement as leverage against the hated NMD. On the first day of the summit, 6 July 2009, the emphasis in media reporting was on the pessimistic side:

> Arms deal could be in peril at summit, says Russia (*Daily Telegraph*)
>
> Missile shield my price for nuclear cutback, Medvedev warns Obama (*Times*)
>
> Russia's tough line on missile shield overshadows Obama's Moscow trip (*Guardian*)

On the next day, the two leaders announced agreement on the arms reduction framework, which they said aimed to achieve cuts of up to a third of US and Russian arms stockpiles, starting from December that year.

> Nuclear mission: Obama and Medvedev in summit pact to scrap more warheads (*Times*)
>
> Thawsome ... US and Russian presidents both vowed to scrap 500 nuclear weapons as a sign of trust (*Sun*)
>
> US and Russia agree nuclear disarmament road map ... Deal could lead to arsenals of both being cut by a third (*Guardian*)
>
> End of the Cold War. Obama and Medvedev heal divisions and sign nuclear weapons pact (*Independent*)

By any measure, this marked a dramatic shift in mood and tone, from talk of irreconcilable differences to historic breakthrough in a matter of days. So what happened to bring it about? Just one item in the media sample gave a clue. This was a report from the *Times* on 8 July 2009, which revealed that, 'President Obama put the Kremlin to the test yesterday by offering to scrap a missile defence shield in Eastern Europe if it helped to stop Iran building a nuclear bomb.' This seemed at the time and on the surface to be a very radical about-turn by the USA for a minor concession from Russia. After all, the NMD issue had remained non-negotiable for well over a decade. The question, then, was why it had become dispensable all of a sudden? It turned out the decision was based on recent US intelligence revealing that Iran's plans for long-range, nuclear weapons capability was moving much slower than first thought and thus presented a much more limited threat to the USA or Europe than what NMD was designed to resist. Obama made the move official on 16 September of that year, finally putting an end to one of the major obstacles to improved US–Russian relations.[1]

On 5 September 2016, Putin met Obama at the margins of the G20 summit in Beijing. The former was over halfway through his third presidency, while the latter was seeing out his last months in office. Putin was being widely criticised, internationally, for Russia's involvement in the Ukrainian conflict, in particular, in 2014, for the annexation of Crimea and the downing of Malaysia Airlines flight MH17 (for analyses of media coverage of both incidents, see Chapter 5). Russia was also suspected of computer hacking to manipulate the US presidential election campaign.

The meeting between the two men, amid deteriorating US–Russian relations, was not going to be easy. Headlines on the next day showed a difference in framing. The popular, right-wing newspapers preferred to see it as a Cold War encounter:

> Tension ... Barack Obama and Vladimir Putin looked like two feuding heavyweights staring each other out (*Express*)
> The new Cold War ... Obama and Putin stare each other out during a frosty meeting (*Sun*)
> On Vlad terms ... Things turned frosty yesterday as Barack Obama and Vladimir Putin exchanged icy glares (*Sun*)

The headlines in the elite newspapers focused on the US-led hacking investigation:

> Obama Warns Putin Against Cyber Arms Race (*Daily Telegraph*)
> US Investigates if Russia may be Trying to Influence Election (*Guardian*)
> US Probes Russian Plans to Sabotage Elections (*Independent*)

Putin denied the hacking allegations but they were to persist and roll into a wider, political scandal in the USA with the election in November that year of Obama's successor: Donald J. Trump.

TRUMP

Donald Trump has been described as a 'disrupter' of political certainty, a man without a political career or evident ideology who suddenly finds himself the leader of the world's only true superpower. On 5 February 2017, he sat down for an interview with Bill O'Reilly, presenter with the right-wing US television channel, Fox News. As with all these set-piece, television encounters with power, the interviewer started off deferential and non-confrontational, an unusual disposition for a man who had garnered a reputation for his pugnacious style. But when the interview turned to the new president's foreign policy agenda and US relations with Russia, this happened:

O'Reilly: Do you respect Putin?
Trump: I do respect him, I ...
O'Reilly: Do you? Why?
Trump: Well, I respect a lot of people but that doesn't mean I'm going to get along with them. He's the leader of his country. I say it's better to get along with Russia than not and if Russia helps us in the fight against ISIS ... and against Islamic terrorism all over the world ... that's a good thing. Will I get along with him? I don't know.
O'Reilly: He's a killer, though! Putin's a killer!
Trump: (Nods) There's a lot of killers. We've got a lot of killers. Why? Do you think our country's so innocent? (Repeats) Do you think our country's so innocent?
O'Reilly: I don't know any leaders who are killers in America.
Trump: Well, take a look at what we've done, too. We've made a lot of mistakes ... there's a lot of killers around, believe me!

The exchange provoked widespread public outrage, especially among the Republican Party establishment that had to date sought to normalise Trump's controversial utterances and behaviour. Trump could insult and sexually assault women, mock disabled people, heap racist insults upon Mexicans, insult the memory of a Muslim US veteran killed in action and threaten journalists: and all with impunity. But keeping an open mind on future relations with President Putin, and drawing moral equivalence between the foreign policies of the USA and Russia, was seen at best, unpatriotic, at worst treasonous. What Trump said in the interview triggered a deeply imbedded ideological tic in the American body politic that transcended party allegiance. Yet, the disrupter did not stop there. Two of his early meetings with Vladimir Putin exploded the predictable ritual of the leaders' summit and how they are understood by the political establishment, the media and the public. The first was at the G20 Summit in Hamburg, Germany, on 7 July 2017; the other was a formal leaders' summit in Helsinki, Finland, 16 July 2018.

Trump's meeting with Putin in Hamburg was certainly his first as US president but it happened amid questions about whether or not he knew Putin or had previously met him before being elected. On the morning of the summit, 7 July 2017, the *Washington Post* reported that up until then, Trump had tweeted about Putin 66 times, going back to 2013. From 2013 to 2016, he boasted on Twitter that he had met and was on good terms with the Russian president. But from the final phase of the US presidential election campaign in 2016, he answered challenges about Russian interference in the Clinton campaign, and the relationship between his election manager and key figures in the Russian government, by denying he had ever met Putin. The issue was to become more critical in the following year at the Helsinki leaders' summit along with growing suspicions that the Russian government might have 'kompromat', incriminating Trump in illegal business dealings in Russia (and a sex tape) and undermining his legitimacy as US president and commander-in-chief of the armed forces.

Personal Dynamics

A media narrative emerged in coverage of the Hamburg Summit, nicknamed 'the Tinder date', that the new president Trump was naive, vulnerable to the lies and the cynical blandishments of Vladimir Putin. This ran counter to what had long become evident about Trump's own cynicism, summed up by his remark during his election campaign that he could shoot someone on 5th Avenue, New York City, and people would still vote for him. Such a narrative was symptomatic of the tendency during that early part of Trump's political career to normalise his behaviour, to explain it away as part of a propaganda campaign to undermine him. The question about Hamburg, then, was: which Trump would prevail?

Reporting for the *Times* (8 July 2017), Tom Parfitt referred to the 'unprecedented' scrutiny being given to the body language between the two presidents as they met on the morning of the summit. Footage of their interaction released by the German government afterwards:

> showed Mr Trump leaning in, grasping Mr Putin by the right hand, then patting the underside of the Russian's forearm briskly three times with his left hand. The US leader patted Mr Putin's back and the Russian leader gestured as he made a comment. Both smiled widely.
>
> (*Times*, 8 July 2017)

By the time of their official bilateral meeting later in the day, 'the mood looked more subdued and business-like' (*Times*, 8 July 2017). The *Times'* editorial on that day looked back in history to the first meeting between presidents Kennedy and Khrushchev in 1961 and how Kennedy came away second best, admitting that the Soviet leader 'just beat the hell out of me'. With that in mind, said the paper, 'Mr Trump was determined to demonstrate strength, not be duped and yet establish a business like tone for the future bilateral relationship' (*Times*, 8 July 2017). In Putin, however, he 'discovered that he was up against a kindred spirit: a thin-skinned politician who trusts nobody and wants to make Russia great again' (*Times*, 8 July 2017). The *Daily Mail* also focused on the body language in an article headlined, 'Eyeball to Eyeball: Trump and Putin in Tense Handshake as They Meet for First Face-to-Face Talks' (*Daily Mail*, 8 July 2017).

Already known for exerting his personal dominance on the world stage, Trump 'abandoned his notorious power handshake' in his meeting with Putin, preferring instead 'a firm shake as they locked eyes', while the Russian president 'put on a show of warmth for the cameras' (*Daily Mail*, 8 July 2017).

Perhaps the most revealing comparisons between the two men came from the liberal *Guardian* in Britain, for reasons rooted in its long-standing hostility to Putin. Trump's populism, his disdain for the EU and NATO, had already raised fears in Europe for the future of the North Atlantic Alliance and, by extension and implication, the international, liberal order that the alliance underpinned. In Britain, these anxieties came against the backdrop of Brexit and the domestic turmoil and division that it was causing. An extraordinary editorial in the *Guardian* (6 July 2017) previewed the meeting, fearing that Vladimir Putin would go into it keen to exploit apparent differences between the USA and its European allies. Its editorial warned that:

> The Russian president is an adept practitioner of mind games. He was schooled in them as a KGB counter-intelligence officer. With the international liberal order shaken by Mr Trump's ascendance, never has so much uncertainty hung over a high-level US–Russia encounter in the post-Soviet era. This reflects Mr Trump's unpredictability as much as Mr Putin's tactics: on the eve of the meeting, even Mr Trump's aides seemed to be in the dark as to what he would do or say.

For the *Guardian*, part of the problem lay in the difference between the two leaders:

> Mr Trump's grasp of complex international issues is limited, to put it mildly, and stands in contrast to the emphatic way Mr Putin likes to demonstrate his mastery of detail. Mr Trump counts on his gut. Mr Putin, who reads intelligence files closely, has a special talent for finessing and outmanoeuvring interlocutors … Mr Putin will sniff out the egomania, and play on the narcissism.

His technique is to give the person he is talking to the impression that he is in agreement, only for it to turn out that his meticulously chosen words carried nuances which amounted in fact to total disagreement.

The other part of the problem, the newspaper thought, was their similarities:

What Mr Trump and Mr Putin do have in common is not encouraging. They are illiberals with a zero-sum game view of the world and utter disdain for democracy. They lie abundantly. They overdo the alpha-male, macho stunts. They target journalists. They associate with ultra-traditionalist, intolerant Christian ideologues … The question is with what goals and what leverage one approaches the Russian president. Mr Putin's hostility to Europe's institutions and values comes with a strategic calculus. Europeans can only hope that Mr Trump will stick to his briefing notes. Mr Putin assumes he won't.

(*Guardian*, 6 July 2017)

In the USA, Democrat, Charles M. Blow, looked back on the Hamburg encounter for the *New York Times* and reminded readers of:

something that you can never allow to become normal and never allow to become acceptable: Our 'president' is a pathological liar. He lies about everything, all the time. Lying is his resting condition. Therefore, absolutely nothing he or his team says is to be believed, ever.

(*New York Times*, 10 July 2017)

The Talks

The bilateral talks were scheduled to last for one hour with an agenda that included the US accusations of Russian meddling in the presidential elections as well as the conduct of Russian air support for the Syrian regime and the Korean nuclear crisis. Also in attendance were the US Secretary of State, Rex Tillerson, the Russian Foreign Minister, Sergei Lavrov, and two translators. In the end, the meeting ran for just over two hours and was followed by contradictory statements to the media on what was discussed in relation to the hacking row. The Americans described a 'robust and lengthy' exchange over the hacking allegations and said that Trump had raised the possibility of sanctions against Russia, if they were proven to be true. The Russians, on the other hand, claimed that Putin had denied the allegations outright and that this was accepted by Trump. For some in the media, it was clear that the Russian president had come out of the talks on top:

> Putin will claim a win from his long talk with Trump ... even if nothing of much substance was discussed with the US leader (*Guardian*, 7 July 2017)
> Did Putin have Trump for Lunch? (*New York Times*, 7 July 2017)
> Russia crows over Putin's meeting with Trump (*New York Times*, 8 July 2017)
> Trump accepts we didn't mess with election, claim Russians (*Times*, 8 July 2017)

But there were also anxieties about what the summit said about the Trump–Putin relationship going into the future. In a column for the *Independent on Sunday* (9 July), David Usborne wrote that:

> Trump let Putin wriggle from the hook in Hamburg. He presumably thinks this will pay off in the longer term if it means the friendship he has sought with the Kremlin can actually take root. As is often the case with Trump, we will have to wait to see if this is bonkers or brilliant, craven or clever.

However, the *Guardian* and the *Daily Mirror* went further to suggest that both leaders presented a challenge to the West. The *Guardian* said that 'the meeting shows two men cut from the same cloth. Both men like to crush dissent and have little time for diplomatic norms – but while the Russian president plays chess with the world, his counterpart just plays' (7 July 2017). In its editorial – headlined, 'Dangerous Duo' – the *Daily Mirror* had this to say of the meeting:

> Better relations between the US and Russia are in the world's interest, but Donald Trump and Vladimir Putin will always be a dangerous odd couple. The pair will never be on an equal footing as long as evidence exists to suggest Putin influenced the US presidential election. Trump's unpredictability and Putin's ruthlessness are frightening – and democracy, freedom and security are the victims. There is a genuine fear in the US that the Kremlin will run rings round the White House, leaving western power compromised. Surely the US and Russia can find leaders we are able to respect rather than loathe?
>
> *(Daily Mirror*, 8 July 2017)

Although this put the onus of fear on Putin and Russia, it was nonetheless an extraordinary characterisation of Trump and suggested something of a paradigm break in Western media framing of an American president and what the office had traditionally symbolised for the West during and since the Cold War: freedom, security and solidarity. However, the second Trump–Putin meeting, in Helsinki, in the following year (16 July 2018), was to provoke not so much a paradigm break but a crisis.

For Trump, the meeting followed a visit to the UK, a country still reeling after the Skripal poisonings, and an uproarious meeting with NATO leaders in Brussels during which he upbraided his allies for not paying enough into the budget. For Putin, it followed a very successful World Cup tournament in Russia but he would not have believed his eyes if he had read the pre-summit headlines, on 16 July 2018, which were dominated by Trump's declaration that the EU was top of America's list of enemies, before even Russia and China:

> America's enemies? The EU is top of the list (*Daily Telegraph*)
> EU is my foe, says Trump before meeting with Putin (*Times*)

Trump: the EU is one of America's greatest foes (*Daily Mail*)

Trump calls European Union a 'foe' – ahead of Russia and China (*Guardian.com*)

When will Europe realise the American president is an antagonist, not an ally? (*Observer*)

Donald Trump is cosying up to Russia and cutting off Europe – be very afraid (*Independent*, 17 July 2018)

Vlad must be purring (*Daily Mirror*)

Concerns about Trump's negative comments about the EU and NATO were quickly drowned out by the media sound and fury that greeted his joint media conference with Putin after their talks. There was some commentary about the optics – Donald throwing Vladimir a wink, Vladimir throwing Donald the gift of an official, world cup football – which seemed to be too cosy against the backdrop of new revelations about Russia's interference in the US presidential election. On 13 July 2018, just a few days before the summit, the US special prosecutor, Robert Mueller, had identified 14 Russian military intelligence agents who he alleged were behind the hacking in 2016 of the Democratic Party's email server. Trump's response to questions about those allegations seemed to subvert expectations of how a US–Russian summit should proceed. Repeating his position from the Hamburg meeting of the previous year, the US president said that he accepted what he called Putin's 'extremely strong and powerful' denial of the allegations. Furthermore, he complained that his relationship with Putin was being undermined by 'American foolishness', specifically that of Mueller's investigation and, more widely, US intelligence agencies. The media response was almost uniformly incredulous and hostile as summed up by this sample of headlines on television that evening and on the following days, starting with a remarkable statement on the Trump-supporting Fox News:

You should call this the surrender summit (John King, Fox News)

Trump sides with Putin over US intelligence (CNN)

Trump sides with Russia against FBI at Helsinki Summit (BBC)

Trump backs Putin over FBI in meddling role (Sky)

Donald Trump under-fire over Putin summit performance (Channel 4 News, 17 July)

Collusion? Backlash after Trump praises Putin in Helsinki (France 24 English, 18 July)

And in the press on 17 July 2018:

Trump backs Putin over FBI in election meddling row (*Daily Telegraph*)

Trump is branded a traitor as he chooses Putin over US spy chiefs (*Times*)

A wink, a handshake ... and a US president accused of treason (*Daily Mail*)

It's Helsinki. Trump summit with Putin. Cheeky hello, then Don backs Vlad (*Sun*)

'Nothing short of treasonous' – Trump accused over Putin talks (*Guardian*)

Bipartisan Outrage as Trump sides with Putin over election meddling (*Independent*)

Trump, at Putin's side, questions US intelligence on 2016 election (*New York Times*)

Trump just colluded with Russia. Openly (*Washington Post*)

Writing in the *Observer* on the eve of the summit, Simon Tisdall worried about the implications of Trump's visit to Europe up until that point:

[He] was busy insulting America's closest friends and threatening to dismember NATO. He publicly humiliated Theresa May and did his importunate best to force regime change in Westminster, before half-heartedly apologising. Now he takes his ugly brand of rogue-male politics to Helsinki for a meeting with his best buddy, prominent campaign supporter and fellow narcissist, Russia's Vladimir Putin.

(*Observer*, 15 July 2018)

In a Europe 'full of fear and loathing', Tisdall asked, 'how far will Trump be allowed to go before leaders of the western democracies finally draw the line? How long until they recognise him as an antagonist, not an ally, contemptuous of their countries' values and interests – and act accordingly?' Invoking George W. Bush's state of the nation address, months after 9/11, he referred to an 'emerging new "axis of evil", linking Trump, Putin and Assad' and wondered if that would be enough for European leaders 'to say enough is enough? War with Iran could make Iraq look like a walk in the park. Yet who, if not us, will stop him [Trump]?' (*Observer*, 15 July 2018). His performance at the media conference that followed put that question front and centre of editorial commentary with unanimous condemnation across the political spectrum, from right to liberal leaning titles.

For the *Times*, Trump was 'facing a backlash from friends and foes, stunned by the spectacle of an American president questioning his own country's competence and integrity' (17 July 2018). On 18 July 2018, the paper said that:

[He] declined to take the word of his own intelligence agencies over that of a foreign ruler ... The president's appeal is largely that he claims to speak as the tribune of the people against a corrupt national elite. Yet when he makes the same accusation standing next to his Russian counterpart he offends American patriotism. Populism does not travel well. It is an alarming basis for foreign policy. The debate in American politics has been for some years how the world's pre-eminent power should react to the coming economic hegemony in the east. Nobody quite foresaw that the American response might be to dismantle the very idea of the West. It will soon be clear that when America chooses to weaken itself, the world is less safe.

(*Times*, 18 July 2018)

The *Daily Mail* reported that he was:

attacked for being 'in the pocket of Putin' ... after he appeared to side with Mr Putin – over his own intelligence agencies – on the issue of Russian interference in the 2016 presidential election ... It prompted a fierce attack from former CIA director John Brennan – who said his behaviour was 'nothing short of treasonous'.

(*Daily Mail*, 17 July 2018)

The *Guardian*'s foreign correspondent and long-time Putin critic, Luke Harding, recalled that: 'For two years, Trump has faced claims that he was beholden to Russia and in some intangible way even controlled by it. Monday's press conference did nothing to banish this impression' (16 July 2018). The paper's editorial noted the US president's pre-summit prediction that his meeting with Putin would be much easier than those in the UK and with NATO in Brussels. In light of what transpired in the summit media conference, it said,

it is clear that this was not an off-the-cuff comment. It was his plan all along. First rough up NATO in order to damage transatlantic commitments, then stir things up in Britain in order to damage the EU, and, finally, play the cooperative statesman in his talks with the Russian president. Or, to put it another way: bully, bully and cringe.

(*Guardian*, 16 July 2018)

The *Guardian* deplored Trump's strategy that:

decries the values that endured in western policy since the defeat of Hitler. It is a conscious break with the post-war network of alliances and aspiration for universal standards. It is a return to the era in which big powers have self-interests not allies ... and international standards are subordinate to military might.

(*Guardian*, 16 July 2018)

Trump's embrace of Russia on the sole basis that it was again a serious military power, said the *Guardian*, might mark the beginning of the end of the Cold War. But there was a worrying, logical extension: that the 'post-1945 order of international values and ethics may be ending too.' Richard Wolffe, a columnist for the *Guardian US*, wrote that watching Trump,

> it was hard to know who was playing the role of the American president. His performance was so nakedly, brazenly pro-Russian, you had to wonder what ranks higher on the Trumpian scale of stupidity: the president's own intellect or his dim view of ours.
>
> (*Guardian*, 16 July 2018)

The *Independent* harked back to the days of the 'old Cold War', when the superpowers – the USA, Russia and China – 'took risks for peace'. Looking at Donald Trump's performance in Helsinki, it saw 'little sign that the risks Mr Trump is staking are actually yielding much of a dividend for anyone. Except Russia' (*Independent*, 17 July 2018). The *Daily Mirror*'s editorial noted that the president 'would accuse any other US president of treason if they sided with Russia against America [but that this] rogue in the White House has a vested interest in dismissing mounting evidence that Vladimir Putin helped him get elected' (16 July 2018). Watching the summit media conference unfold, the paper thought that, 'Putin must be purring with satisfaction that his poodle [Trump] is destroying the American republic from the inside.' Donald J. Trump, it concluded, was 'Putin's dream president and America's worst nightmare' (*Daily Mirror*, 16 July 2018).

The reaction among columnists and pundits in the USA, not surprisingly, was one of shock and disgust. From that perspective, the office of the president is meant to symbolise everything that is great about the country as the world's only true superpower. Of course, the office is about more than symbolism. It carries extensive executive power, including (as in Russia) over matters of national defence such as the power to order the launch of nuclear missiles and to command access to the highest levels of foreign and domestic intelligence. So to watch Donald Trump cosy up to the traditional old enemy of the USA, and take its word against that of his own police and intelligence agencies, was not in the summit script.

Writing in the *New York Times* online (16 July 2018), Thomas Friedman called Trump's behaviour

> so perverse, so contrary to American interests and values, that it leads to only one conclusion: Donald Trump is either an asset of Russian intelligence or really enjoys playing one on TV ... There is overwhelming evidence that our president, for the first time in our history, is deliberately or through gross negligence, or because of his own twisted personality, engaged in treasonous behavior – behavior that violates his oath of office to 'preserve, protect and defend the Constitution of the United States'.
>
> (*New York Times*, online, 16 July 2018)

The *Washington Post* condemned Trump's acceptance of Putin's denial and, more to the point, his 'groundless attack on the FBI' (16 July 2018). In front of a global audience, 'Trump appeared to align himself with the Kremlin against American law enforcement before the Russian ruler' and issue 'a series of statements that could have been scripted in Moscow.' The editorial concluded that 'in refusing to acknowledge the plain facts about Russia's behavior, while trashing his own country's justice system, Mr. Trump in fact was openly colluding with the criminal leader of a hostile power' (*Washington Post*, 16 July 2018). In the *New Yorker* (16 July 2018), Joshua Yaffa declared himself 'shocked but not surprised' by Trump's demeanour at the media conference,

> because it has been clear for some time that, at a minimum, Trump has a kind of autocrat's envy for Putin, who is the strongman that Trump likes to play on television, and, at a maximum, may feel beholden to him or the Russian state and those close to it.
>
> (*New Yorker*, 16 July 2018)

There was no doubt, he said, that Putin came out on top in Helsinki and 'must be flying back to Moscow content, not because he did anything so skillful or brilliant ... but because he was simply smart enough to sit back and pocket one good hand after another' (*New Yorker*, 16 July 2018).

For the Western media, part of the sensation about the Trump–Putin summits, Slovenia in 2017 and Helsinki in 2018, lay in the apparent similarities in personalities between the two leaders. Both men appeared to be narcissistic, power hungry and obsessed with making their county 'great again'. But the differences were probably more crucial than the similarities and those lie in between Trump's weaknesses and Putin's strengths. A good illustration of this can be found in the contrast between public appearances in 2016. As the US presidential campaign reached its peak in August that year, Trump appeared at a supporters' rally in Ohio and, with his full range of grotesque grimaces and hand gestures, had this to say about the president of Russia:

Putin called me a genius! Putin said Donald Trump is a genius! Putin said good things about me. He said that he's a leader. There's no question about it! He's a genius! I love you all! Thank you![2]

At the end of the year, in Moscow, Vladimir Putin held his annual conferences with the international media (23 December 2016). Cool and imperious from start to finish, he fielded the full range of questions covering domestic and foreign policy before the event ended with a strange question from an unidentified journalist:

Reporter: Can I ask you a question about love?
Vladimir Putin: Love quickly turns to hate.
(*Guardian.com*, 23 December 2016)

Putin delivered his reply with the cold flourish of a signature on an executive order but there is no evidence that he was alluding to international relations and how fickle they could be. However, it did reveal a self-confidence of leadership and power that Donald Trump did not seem to radiate on the campaign trail.

On 1 March 2018, just two weeks before the Russian presidential election, Vladimir Putin gave a state of the nation address in

Moscow, which took a strange and unexpected turn when he gave a PowerPoint show on a new range of nuclear arms being developed for Russia's arsenal. This was a mix of video footage of missiles launching and animations showing them leaving the earth's atmosphere before launching their payloads of nuclear warheads. At one point, it showed several such warheads targeting what looked to the international media to be southern Florida, the location of Donald Trump's holiday resort. There was much laughter from the audience at that one, with Putin allowing himself a wry smile, but as the *Guardian* pointed out, Florida is also the location of the US military's central command (1 March 2018). The media headlines on the next day emphasised the 'shock and awe' effect that Putin was evidently intending:

> Putin: my nuclear bombs cannot be stopped (*Daily Telegraph*)
> 'My rockets are bigger and faster', boasts Putin (*Times*)
> Chilling threat of Putin: Russia's new nuclear missiles are invincible (*Daily Mail*)
> Putin unveils 'untraceable' nuke (*Daily Express*)
> Putin on blitz: Vlad's 'unstoppable' nuke new weapons threat to US (*Sun*)
> Putin on the blitz: Vlad's big nukes boast (*Daily Star*)
> Putin's nuclear slideshow reveals Russia's naked ambitions (*Guardian*, 2 March)
> Vlad's invincible nuke (*Daily Mirror*)
> Putin's 'invincible' missile is aimed at US vulnerabilities (*New York Times*)

Behind the headlines, however, was the question of who the show of arms was aimed at and why. The preferred interpretation was that it was meant as a direct warning to the USA, which had only a month earlier announced its own plans for a new generation of nuclear weapons.[3] If understood in this context, this was a tit-for-tat, propaganda competition between two hawkish leaders but one which could have serious implications for nuclear arms control (*Times*, *Guardian*, *Independent*, *Daily Mirror* and *New York Times*). The

Guardian also raised another possibility that Putin was looking ahead to the imminent presidential election, with his slide in the opinion polls foremost in his mind (2 March 2018). 'It may all have been bluff and braggadocio', said the newspaper, 'but Russia's president has little else left to motivate voters' (*Guardian*, 2 March 2018). And, in the *Independent*, Mary Dejevsky interpreted the show as a call for attention, 'more a plea to the US to start talking again, on the basis of mutual respect.'

Donald Trump's performance at the Helsinki Summit seemed typical of his status as a 'disrupter', taking the side of an enemy against his country's intelligence agencies and handing him a tactical advantage. Yet, three months later, he caught observers offside again when he announced that the USA would withdraw from the Intermediate-Range Nuclear Forces (INF) Treaty, signed by presidents Ronald Reagan and Mikhail Gorbachev in 1987 and regarded by many commentators at the time as 'a landmark' agreement on arms control.

INF WITHDRAWAL

The INF Treaty obliged the two superpowers to implement significant reductions of their stocks of medium-range nuclear missiles. It was welcomed especially in Western Europe, where governments feared that such weapons assumed the possibility of fighting and deciding a nuclear war in Europe. Thirty years later, the US announcement of its intent to withdraw from the treaty would inevitably provoke a reciprocal move from Russia and open the way for a dangerous new arms race by effectively neutering subsequent treaties to reduce and limit strategic, long-range nuclear forces (the START agreements). Donald Trump first let it be known on 20 October 2018 that the USA may withdraw from the treaty unless Russia ceased developing weapons that contravened the spirit, if not the letter of the INF Treaty. The response in the Western media was not a simple split between liberal media, who saw it as yet another example of Donald Trump's threat to international order, and conservative media who saw it as a move provoked by Russian bad faith. In other words, such readings were not determined by the traditional editorial position of particular media outlets. This might explain the ambivalence in media analyses between old Cold War certainties and a measure of confusion about Donald Trump's personality flaws vis-à-vis his ever-changing policy positions.

Take the initial media reactions to Trump's initial announcement. In the *Times*, the ubiquitous Putin/Russia critic, Edward Lucas, presented an analysis, headlined, 'Paranoia is the Religion of Putin's Russia. We should not pander to the Kremlin's desire to paint itself as the victim of foreign ill will' (22 October 2018). Lucas was critical of the US threat to tear up the agreement, calling it 'a particularly big mistake [that would] make life a lot more dangerous. So too would building a big stockpile here of hair-trigger nuclear weapons, as some Americans [and defence contractors] would like' (*Times*, 22 October 2018). This, he argued, would bring out the very worst of Putin. Referring to the Russian leader's 'alarming tendency to talk loosely about nuclear weapons', he said that Trump's warning would only reinforce the conviction in Moscow 'that American missile defence installations in Europe have made the treaty obsolete and (so in response) is developing an alarming ground-launched cruise missile in direct breach of its rules' (*Times*, 22 October 2018). The threat to withdraw, he concluded, would also:

> incense European opinion, and prompt just the transatlantic row that the Kremlin seeks. A nuclear arms race would stoke Russia's siege mentality, giving the regime new excuses to crack down and lash out. It also makes Russia look more important than it is.
>
> (*Times*, 22 October 2018).

In a similar vein, Mark Almond in the *Daily Mail* predicted that Trump's announcement would provoke criticism from America's European allies. While he 'has declared he wants to make America safer … my fear is that he has made the world an even more dangerous place' (22 October 2018). However, as with Lucas, the real danger for Almond appeared to be the Russian president. Sowing division between the USA and its European allies would suit Putin perfectly 'because it plays into his divide-and-rule approach to Europe' (*Daily Mail*, 22 October 2018). Furthermore, the type of weapons Putin had promised in his presentation, in March 2018, would put the allies directly in the firing line of an enemy with little else to lose:

> Today's Kremlin boss is ruthless, but worse he runs a Russia much less moribund than the wheezing Communist colossus of the 1980s. Putin's armed forces are much leaner and meaner than in those days. War in the 21st century has been practised already from Syria to Ukraine and in cyberspace. Putin knows he doesn't need two million badly trained soldiers to be sacrificed in the trenches.
>
> (*Daily Mail*, 22 October 2018)

In an editorial headlined, 'Trump has Eroded What Little Trust was Left Between the US and Russia', the liberal *Independent* nonetheless pointed to skulduggery on the Russian front:

> The Russians are engaged in a campaign of territorial expansion once more, pushing at the Baltic states and the EU where it sees weakness. The digital age has brought new channels of cyber warfare and surveillance. Russians now use ... chemical weapons ... on the streets of Britain. At home, too, Russia has returned to an internal culture of repression and authoritarianism. It has not (yet) regressed to full-on paranoid Stalinism, but it is developing its own modern brand of near dictatorship, which we might term Putinism ... It is smarter and less brutal than its antecedents, but no less ruthless.
>
> (*Independent*, 22 October 2018)

On 1 February 2019, the USA gave its official, six-month notice to withdraw from the INF Treaty unless Russia scrapped its new range of missiles and launchers that it said breached the agreement. Russia responded in kind and promised to continue development. Some headlines in the media, conservative and liberal, framed the mutual withdrawal as a passive abandonment by the USA versus an aggressive response by Putin and/or Russia:

> Putin signals restart of nuclear weapons programme. Russia follows US in pulling out of disputed arms treaty and threatens new range of missiles (*Sunday Telegraph*, 3 February)
>
> Putin threatens to revive arms race as US abandons treaty (*Sunday Times*, 3 February)
>
> Russia pulls out of nuclear deal after US suspends treaty (*Sun*, 3 February)
>
> Putin pulls out of nuclear weapons treaty and orders new missiles to be built. Russian president is copying US withdrawal from the deal (*Independent on Sunday*, 3 February)
>
> Russia plans land-based intermediate missiles in two years. Defence minister instructs military to develop missiles following collapse of US–Russia nuclear weapons treaty (*Guardian*, 5 February)
>
> Russia to create hypersonic land-based missile systems. Putin takes step after Trump pulls out of nuclear arms treaty (*Independent*, 6 February)

Others reported it as it was – a US action prompting a Russian reaction – and focused on the dangers of a new arms race and a new Cold War. In the *Mail on Sunday*, Michael Burleigh reminded readers that it was not the first time that Donald Trump left an international agreement, an allusion to the Paris climate agreement (2016), but

> his decision to withdraw from the long-standing Intermediate-Range Nuclear Forces treaty with Russia is a milestone – and a disturbing one. After all, this is the treaty that helped bring the Cold War to a close ... There is no doubting that the INF treaty made the world a safer place.
>
> (*Mail on Sunday*, 3 February 2019)

Describing Trump's claim that Russia had been cheating on the terms of the treaty as 'bogus and hypocritical', Burleigh pointed to the US deployment of missile defence systems in Poland and Romania, despite the promise by Trump's predecessor, Obama, to scrap these. There was also America's fleet of drones, weapons that did not exist when the INF Treaty was signed in 1988, but which appeared to breach the underlying assumptions of the agreement. What, then, he asked, was the real reason behind the withdrawal? Burleigh argued that it was the fear of China, which was not a signatory to the INF Treaty and therefore not bound by its restrictions and limitations. Put quite simply, the INF Treaty restricted the USA's ability to challenge and limit China's power in the Pacific. But most worryingly of all are the implications for the future. With the New START agreement on long-range missiles coming up for renewal in 2021, a re-elected Trump might well dump that, too: 'Then we would truly be heading back to a new Cold War – an era in which mass destruction is but a push of a button away' (*Mail on Sunday*, 3 February 2019).

CONCLUDING REMARKS

The media's universally negative response to Trump's performance at the Helsinki Summit was in one way exceptional when compared with the meetings between previous American presidents and Vladimir Putin as sampled in this chapter. But, of course, Trump survived the public outrage, when any of his predecessors might have faced calls for resignations or even faced the threat of impeachment had they taken the side of a foreign leader against their own country's intelligence apparatus. In that context, media anxieties about the Trump–Putin relationship might only represent a paradigm anomaly rather than a paradigm rupture. With this in mind, Chapter 7, the next and final chapter examines media discourse about whether or not we are seeing a return to a cold war between the West and Russia.

7

The Makings of a New Cold War?

This book has examined media coverage of Vladimir Putin and Russia at key moments since Putin emerged as the real power, in 1999. It has shown how the media, particularly in Britain, established from the beginning a very clear enemy image of the Russian leader, and one that was sometimes inflated to an extent bordering on hysteria mixed with comic-book caricature. He was 'the ex-KGB man', the 'mob boss', the 'unrepentant Cold War warrior', the 'narcissist', the 'ruthless' war leader, the 'cold fish' and much more besides (see the full Putin Lexicon of terms in Appendix A). This contrasted to the use of language in the *New York Times*, America's 'newspaper of record', which conformed to its tradition of objectivity, eschewing pejoratives and referring to him, even in incidents of high international tension, such as the war in Georgia, formally as the 'President of Russia, Mr Vladimir S. Putin' or variants thereof. In an interview for this book, Mary Dejevsky of the *Independent* sees this as 'a reflection of the UK press being especially politicised by international standards and the USA having this supposed wall between news and comment'.[1] However, she has noticed a certain breakdown in that separation in recent times with particular respect to 'Russia-gate', that is, Russia's interference in the US presidential election in 2016. Even so, she agrees that coverage of Putin in the British press has sometimes descended to demonisation, a pattern that was set at a very early stage in the 'Putin story':

> I have tried to point this out and contest it since what seems like whenever. But the prevailing sentiment – less in the media, I would say, than in the 'establishment' – has left very little room for other views. Part of it started, I would say, very early on, when a combination of Berezovsky, the Chechen War, and the presence

of leading Chechens in London successfully courted the political and arts elite.[2]

She goes further to argue that in Britain, the *Guardian* has played a key role in leading this very negative coverage of Russia:

> The press may seem more monolithic recently than in the past because the *Guardian* has essentially changed sides on Russia. It used to be – in the days of Jonathan Steele *et al.* – friendly to the Soviet Union and then to Russia. When Luke Harding was Moscow correspondent and then when his visa was not renewed (he was not expelled, she points out), the *Guardian* became as hostile to Russia as almost everyone else. Since returning to the UK, Luke has led the coverage of Litvinenko (ref. Harding, 2016), Russia-gate ('collusion'), and the Skripals, which has left no mainstream outlet offering any other view. I have had occasional dissenting views published in the *Guardian* and managed a contrary line on Litvinenko and the Skripals in the *Independent*. But that is now online only, and mine is generally not the paper's editorial line.[3]

But the mobilisation of the enemy image, however it might be coloured by subjective language, does not in itself signify the existence of a Cold War framework akin to that which was used to interpret or explain East–West relations throughout much of the twentieth century. What it has done has been to function as a form of propaganda or a rhetorical weapon in itself, as a stick to beat Putin and resurgent, post-Soviet Russia, often distracting from the West's role triggering tension, sometimes even exacerbating it. For example, on a rational level, Russia's objections to NATO expansion eastwards to its 'near abroad', and the USA plans to roll out its missile defence system (NMD) in former World Trade Organization countries, such as Poland and the Czech Republic, can be understood as an attitude of national self-interest or a legitimate grievance. Yet, within the Western propaganda framework, it is explained as an attitude of unreasonable and inexplicable paranoia, 'typical' of Putin and his regime.

Also, as shown throughout this book, the enemy image has often been driven by a dependency on various correspondents, contributors or pundits long hostile to Putin since his rise to power. Indeed, any historical study of Western propaganda during the old Cold War would recognise that media constructions of the Soviet Union as 'the enemy' were never driven by traditional media politics, by the assumption that conservative media would be hostile to, and the liberal media more sympathetic of, the Soviet state and the communist project. To recall Edward Thompson's definition in Chapter 2, the Cold War had deeper, ideological structures than the political or even class allegiances that defined the West's system of parliamentary democracy and representation. By extension, Cold War propaganda went beyond the enemy image to serve as a consistent, interpretative framework to explain and define the conflict. As by way of a conclusion, then, this chapter will examine whether the 'New Cold War' narratives that have defined media coverage of Putin and Russia represent something structural or paradigmatic, a framework that goes beyond personalities or moments of conflict to something deeper and more long term.

COLD WAR TALK

Chapter 5 of this book examined media coverage of Russia's wars in Chechnya, Georgia, Ukraine and Crimea, and its involvement in the Syrian Civil War in support of President Assad. In all but the case of Syria, the media framed Russian actions within a wider question of whether they represented the makings of a new Cold War with the danger of a global, nuclear conflict in the future or if they were more typical of the Great Power gambits of the nineteenth century.

With Prime Minister Vladimir Putin taking charge of the Second Chechen War in 1999, his president, Boris Yeltsin, travelled to China in December that year. In serious decline with ill health, Yeltsin chose the occasion to hit back at the USA's criticism of Russia's war in Chechnya with a reminder that his country was still a nuclear power and should be respected as such on the world stage. The *New York Times* responded with headlines such as 'A Bristling Yeltsin Reminds Clinton of Russia's A-Arms', 'Boris Yeltsin's Outburst', and 'Yeltsin Waves Saber at West', yet put more store in Putin's reassurances that Russia wanted to maintain good relations with the West; the implied message being that Yeltsin's days were numbered and that the real power in the land lay with Putin. The reaction among some of the British media was rather more heightened and sensationalised:

My Finger is Still on the Button, Boris Warns West (*Express*, 9 December)

Yeltsin gives US Nuclear Warning (*Guardian*, 10 December)

Yeltsin the Defiant Rattles Nuclear Sabre (*Daily Mail*, 10 December)

Remember Bill, We've Still Got Nuke Bombs. Yeltsin's Chechnya Warning (*Daily Mirror*, 10 December)

Boris 'Is Bonkers' (*Daily Mirror*, 15 December)

Even as Yeltsin resigned in the new year and Putin stepped into a provisional role until the presidential election proper in March 2000, the *Mail on Sunday* reported the changeover within the frame of the nuclear weapons threat: 'Putin gets nuclear button. New hardman takes control with a pledge to crush the Chechens' (2 January 2000). The spectre of nuclear confrontation appeared again in 2008 when Russian forces entered Georgia. The USA chose the moment to announce a putative deal with Poland to host part of its missile defence system. In response, a senior Russian army officer warned that according to the logic of nuclear doctrine, this would make Poland an obvious target for a Russian strike in the event of a nuclear war. The propaganda that ensued defined Western media coverage of the Russo–Georgian War, with the Russian warning presented in headlines and reports as a real, even imminent threat to a Western ally:

Could This be the Most Dangerous Flashpoint Since the Cuba Crisis? (*Daily Mail*, 9 August)

The West must Take Heed as Russia Shows its Claws Again
(*Sunday Express*, 10 August)
Russia Lashes Out on Missile Deal (*New York Times*, 15 August)
Russia Nuclear Strike Threat (*Daily Telegraph*, 16 August)
Russia in Nuclear Threat to Poland (*Times*, 16 August)
Moscow Turns Up Heat with a Nuclear Warning (*Daily Mail*, 16
August)
We'll Nuke Poland (*Sun*, 16 August)
Moscow Warns it Could Strike Poland over US Missile Shield
(*Guardian*, 16 August)
Moscow Issues Nuclear Warning to Poland (*Independent*, 16
August)
The New Cold War Hots Up (*Sunday Times*, 17 August)
Russia's New Nuclear Challenge to Europe (*Sunday Times*, 17
August)

Russia's involvement in the nationalist conflict in Ukraine and its
annexation of the Crimea, in 2014, also provoked headlines using
explicit Cold War references:

Russia and NATO face off over Ukraine (*Daily Telegraph*, 27
February)
The Crisis in Crimea Could Lead the World into a second Cold
War (*Observer*, 2 March)
Europe's Peace at Risk in New Cold War (*Daily Mail*, 3 March)
Don't Mess with the Bear (*Sunday Telegraph*, 9 March)
And so the Cold War Starts Again (*Sunday Times*, 16 March)
Mr Putin and the Threat of a new Cold War (*Guardian*, 17 March)
Strutting Putin Stokes a New Cold War as Crimea Returns to the
Fold (*Times*, 19 March)
Crimea 'Could Spark a New Cold War' (*Daily Express*, 19 March)

While NATO could observe only limited Russian troop movements
near the border with Ukraine, the *Daily Mail*, reported otherwise. It
picked up a grossly exaggerated warning from 'a senior security chief
in Kiev', that the Russian army was about to invade, and headlined

it as fact: 'Red Army Masses on Ukraine Border' (*Daily Mail*, 13 March 2014). The use of the title 'Red Army' here evoked a powerful Cold War image: that of a massive, military force overwhelming the Western world, destroying democracy and imposing the evil ideology of communism on state after state.

An intriguing feature of media coverage of Russia's support for President Assad in Syria was the relative absence of the Cold War rhetoric that marked the reporting of Chechnya, Georgia and the Crimea. In fact, only nine out of the 220 items in the sample featured Cold War references. Of these, six saw relations between Russia and the West as merely reminiscent of the Cold War of the past. For example, the *Guardian* noted that Russia's intervention in Syria was its first 'major military action outside the borders of the former Soviet Union since the end of the cold war' (17 March 2016), while the *Mirror* described Russia's assault on Aleppo from November 2016 as 'its largest military surface deployment since the Cold War' (1 November 2016). After the election of Donald Trump as US president, Putin was one of the first world leaders to congratulate him with a very friendly phone call. In an editorial headed, 'The Danger of Going Soft on Russia', the *New York Times* worried that:

> Just when relations between Russia and the West are at their most precarious point since the Cold War, Mr. Trump has been Russia's defender and the beneficiary of Moscow's efforts to influence the presidential campaign. [...] Even so, the relationship between the United States and Russia cannot be allowed to slip back into a poisonous Cold War-like rivalry.
>
> (*New York Times*, 12 November 2016)

In Britain, the *Guardian* interpreted the relationship as one between the old Cold War superpowers rather than between leaders (29 December 2016). In the war in Syria, and in the wider Middle East, it said, 'It is Moscow and not Washington that is calling the shots':

> Reeling from its cold war defeat and the subsequent collapse of the Soviet empire, Moscow was unable to save Yugoslavia from

what it termed western aggression. But in the case of Syria, it can claim it has recovered its self-respect. In the process, it has built a brutal reputation for sticking by its friends, understanding the dynamics of the region better than America, and knowing how to use military power to forge diplomatic alliances.

(*Guardian*, 29 December 2016)

Only three items asserted that a new Cold War was in the making. Edward Lucas, author of the book, *The New Cold War* (2014), wrote in the *Daily Mail* that:

The restoration of the Soviet empire is under way and America is not going to stop it ... Without the weight of America to hold it together, the West, squabbling, weak-willed and ill-led, is now easy prey for the Kremlin.

(*Daily Mail*, 17 November 2016)

For Charles Moore in the *Daily Telegraph*,

Under Putin ... Russia has made itself once again the enemy of the West [...] He cheats; we bleat; so he cheats again. [...] But the point is that he knows what he is doing and we don't know what we're doing.

(*Daily Telegraph*, 16 December 2016)

And writing in the *Guardian* in response to Russia's initial intervention, Natalie Nougayrède argued that:

by rekindling a US–Russia duality reminiscent of the cold war – or at least the pretence of it – Putin calculates that the ultimate geopolitical prize will come not in the Middle East but in Europe. That is where Russia's historical obsessions truly lie.

(*Guardian*, 18 March 2016)

These allusions back to the Cold War expose a certain loss of first-hand knowledge and experience of the Cold War in contemporary journalism. This is certainly the view of Mary Dejevsky, who reported from Moscow on the end of the Soviet Union in 1991:

> I think the problem with the 'New Cold War' term was that a lot of those using it actually had no idea what the real Cold War was like and no appreciation of how Russia/Soviet Union was at that time, so it was a rather nebulous idea rather than anything more. I think that coexisted with the Great Power/Great Game ideas, with journalists maybe trying to couch the situation in terms they thought readers would understand.[4]

Deploying frightening headlines about nuclear war and Cold War in response to the behaviour of an ill and drunk Russian president Yeltsin in 1999, the logic of a senior Russian general in 2008, or the opportunism of Putin in Crimea, was a propaganda response to Russia taking military action outside its own borders. According to the script of the post-Cold War order, such action appeared to be permissible for the West but not permissible for Russia. Indeed, the outrage in the West about Russia's invasion of Georgia came with no sense of irony, coming as it did just five years after the illegal invasion of Iraq. But behind the headlines, the comment and opinion pages allowed for rather more considered responses that for the most part rejected the idea that the world was entering a new Cold War. What emerges from an analysis of this content is an argument for an era that would see something more like the Great Power game of the nineteenth century, of imperial containment and competition. There would be wars but without nuclear confrontation. This kind of 'puzzling through' was most concentrated and intense in the coverage of the Russo–Georgian War (2008), therefore the following analysis takes that as its basis.

GREAT POWER GAMES

But the cartoon images in the Western media of 'the angry bear … stretching out a claw to maul Georgia' was not the most accurate or revealing. The *Times* described Russia's victory in Georgia as 'brutal

– and brilliant … What the world has seen last week is a brilliant and brutal display of Russia's national game, chess. And Moscow has just declared checkmate' on the West (14 August 2008). In the *Daily Telegraph*, the conservative columnist, Anne Applebaum, describes the conflict between the West and Russia as 'not exactly a new Cold War, but an unavoidable, possibly very long-term ideological battle with Russia, above and beyond the normal economic and political competition' (15 August 2008). This would require a rethink of 'what it means to be "the West", and about how Western institutions … can be brought into the 21st century, not merely to counter terrorism, but to argue the case for Western values, once again' (*Daily Telegraph*, 15 August 2008). Reporting from Tbilisi, the Georgian capital, for the newspaper on the following day, Adam Blomfield argued that 'talk of a new Cold War is growing ever louder. Yet, even now, that description is fallacious, not least because history rarely replicates itself so precisely' (*Daily Telegraph*, 16 August 2008). Russia had no longer an ideology to export and it lacked the military power and reach of the old Soviet Union. This, he said, '[did] not mean that Russia is not a dangerous foe … [Any] country with such a large stockpile of nuclear weapons and so voluminous a supply of energy (on which Europe is increasingly dependent), is a foe to be reckoned with.' While the 'theatre of international relations will have the scenery of the Cold War … the play being staged is much more likely to resemble the Great Power diplomacy of the 19th century' (*Daily Telegraph*, 16 August 2008). And the author, Edward Luttwak, warned in the *Sunday Telegraph* that Russia's 'reversion … to the dangerous rules of great-power politics compels all other countries to change their behaviour as well. Unfortunately, this is not a game, and participation is not voluntary' (17 August 2008).

The argument against Western provocation was also presented by Stephen Glover in the *Daily Mail* under the headline, 'Shamed by the Loss of Empire, Russia is a Wounded Bear we Provoke at our Grave Peril' (11 August 2008). He opened with the dismissal of the parallels some were making between Russia's invasion of Georgia and the Soviet Union's interventions in Hungary (1956) and Czechoslovakia (1968); and, indeed, those being made between Russia and the Soviet Union. Russia was 'a country that has undergone extreme psychological trauma since the Soviet empire broke up nearly 20 years ago'; and, in the face of Western expansionism, 'has developed some paranoid tendencies'. Yet, Glover ended,

> none of this makes her a looming threat to the security of the West or reopens the Cold War. Russia is not the Soviet Union, and don't believe those politicians or pundits who imply that she is. [...] We can persist in seeing Russia as a bear if we like, but she is a caged one, as well as somewhat wounded, and there is nothing to be gained from poking sticks through her bars.
>
> (*Daily Mail*, 11 August 2008)

In the *Guardian*, Mark Almond rejected the 'cold war reflex' driving Western responses to the invasion including the simplistic narrative about 'Plucky little Georgia' being put down like Hungary and Czechoslovakia. He argued instead that it had 'more in common with the Falklands war of 1982 than it does with a cold war crisis' (*Guardian*, 9 August 2008). In the *Daily Mail*, the former war correspondent, Max Hastings wrote that: 'A worldwide contest will dominate the 21st century, very different from the Cold War, but almost as frightening for us ... in a vastly more confused "multi-polar" world' (16 August 2008).

In its editorial of 17 August 2008, 'Controlling the New Russia Requires New Thinking', the *Observer* argued that Russia's invasion, and the West's response to it, might look like 'old-fashioned Cold War escalation', but the difference this time was that 'the economic ties binding the two sides are stronger'. Russia's desire for access to Western markets and Europe's dependence on Russian gas opened the opportunity for the European Union to 'play a moderating role, steering the conversation away from military grandstanding and towards economic negotiation'. In that regard, said the *Observer*, 'Brussels, not Washington ... stands the best chance of persuading Moscow to change its ways'. Adrian Hamilton, in the *Indepen-*

dent, described the West's response to the end of the Cold War as 'muddle-headed' (14 August 2008). While it accused Russia 'of reverting to the behaviour of the past, it is Washington and London that have in fact continued the Cold War mindset.' The West's attitude since the end of the Cold War was to march triumphantly eastwards and lock a humiliated Russia into isolation. While there was no doubting the challenges that the new, resurgent Russia posed, the West would only meet those by deciding on 'what it is that we represent and what our associations are for ... It's not the Cold War we're returning to, but the bitty, brutal and shifting world of the 19th century. Only we don't have the gunboats to control it' (*Independent*, 14 August 2008). For the same newspaper, Rupert Cornwell wondered what George Kennan would have made of the situation in Georgia (*Independent*, 16 August 2008). Kennan was the renowned American diplomat who, in the early years of the Cold War, established the 'containment' doctrine that was to steer US policy on the Soviet Union decades thereafter. Would he 'conclude that history has gone on a 60-year fast rewind, and that the Cold War is back? The answer is an unequivocal no.' As 'unlovable' as Russia was under Vladimir Putin, it was 'no longer the world-wide ideological adversary of the West, using proxy wars on four continents to advance its cause.' And even though it was asserting itself as a rival of the USA, it was not its most 'mortal adversary in a 21st century reincarnation of the Cold War'. Russia's actions and its assertive posture had to be assessed in the context of prevailing 'global realities', Cornwell went on, which included a much weaker USA. Far from a new Cold War,

> What we are witnessing is a reversion to pre-20th century great-power politics, featuring not just a somewhat creaky US and a resurgent Russia, but emerging actors such as China, India and, who knows, maybe Europe as well. In Moscow's case, its current great-power behaviour is fuelled by resentment and a desire for payback, after the humiliations of the Yeltsin era – on a playing field that is now tilted in its direction.
>
> (*Independent*, 16 August 2008)

CONCLUDING REMARKS

In a sample of nearly 500 news items on the very short-lived Russo–Georgian War, only two featured a critical analysis of the West's policy and, by implication, the underlying narrative assumptions of Western media coverage. This was in 2008, just as the war in Georgia was reaching its end game. In an article for the *Daily Mail*, 'NATO is Pushing Russia into a New Cold War', Andrew Alexander argued that 'the Americans are proving a menace on the international stage. And the term humbug is wholly inadequate to describe the reproaches that President Bush heaps on the Russians' (15 August 2008). Alexander questioned George Bush's proposals to base his national missile defence system in Poland and the Czech Republic. But it was his promotion of NATO expansion eastwards to Russia's borders that seemed most historically insensitive and dangerous. 'Almost beyond belief,' he wrote,

NATO is wooing the Ukraine. Yet, as anyone with an ounce of history knows, fear of encirclement has characterised Russia for centuries [and] has a deep hold on the country's psyche. This is not just being ignored by the U.S., it is being flouted.

(Daily Mail, 15 August 2008)

Moreover, NATO was 'the principal cause' of the decline in East–West relations since the end of the Cold War and its drive eastwards 'fitted all too well with Washington's expansionist instincts.' The policy of provoking Russia, he concluded, was leaving the world 'in a position as if the Cold War had never ended.' It was 'not only dangerous [but] wholly unnecessary. Russia will do as it pleases ... when it thinks its own security is at stake. It is hard to see why President Bush, of all people, should be surprised, let alone shocked' (*Daily Mail*, 15 August 2008).

In her column for the *Independent*, on the same day, 'Russia the bad guys? Who is the West trying to kid?', Mary Dejevsky argued that the Western media narrative of the conflict, 'that the US faced down a snarling, expansionist Russia, and forced it to limp back to its lair (was) a travesty' (15 August 2008). This, she wrote, was just 'the latest and most glaring in a series of Western misrepresentations and mis-readings of Russian intentions throughout this sorry episode.' Russia did what it said it was going to do from the start – to assert its right to South Ossetia so, she asked, 'does it matter that its intentions were so appallingly misread? Yes it does.' As long as the West read the worst in Russian actions, 'they alienate Russia even further, and make a long-term solution of many international problems that more difficult.' It was time to treat 'Russia's post-Soviet leaders as responsible adults representing a legitimate national interest, rather than assuming the stereotypical worst' (*Independent*, 15 August 2008).

And that is the problem with how the media in the West have treated Putin and his regime in Russia. Since Putin's rise to ultimate power in Russia in 2000, he has been seen by the West and its media as a 'problem' that can only be controlled and opposed. He is an authoritarian who has locked down freedom and democracy in Russia; who has used his country's energy resources to bully and cajole the EU into keeping its distance while, at the same time, taking opportunities to assassinate opponents at home and abroad; and who has conducted wars in Chechnya, Georgia and Ukraine in its 'near abroad' and assisted Syria in its war against 'freedom fighters' as a means to assert his authority on the international scene. Yet there is much less attention paid to the West's policy on Russia in the same period: to how it has interfered in Russia's near abroad, namely, Georgia and Ukraine; or to how the USA, for example, has used its power over Poland and the Czech Republic to develop a missile system as a counterweight against Iran, North Korea, ISIS and other unidentified threats without specifying Russia. There is little in the way of a more rational paradigm of discourse, and there may never be one until Putin stands down in 2024.

Appendix A
The Putin Lexicon

BRITISH NEWSPAPER DESCRIPTIONS OF PRESIDENT PUTIN,
2000–2018: CHAPTERS 3–7
(Frequency of more than one occurrence in brackets)

Action man (3)
Afraid
Aggressive
Alpha male
Ambitious
Another Stalin
Anti-democrat (2)
Apolitical
Archetypal secret policeman
Authoritarian (3)
Autocrat

Bland
Bogeyman
Brutal (3)
Brutish
Bully (3)
Business-like

Calculating
Calm (2)
Calm decisiveness
Canny
Chairman of the world's unofficial Autocrat's Club
Cheat

Classic Bond villain
Cold
Cold-eyed ruler
Cold-eyed former spy
Cold fish
Competitive
Confident
Contemptuous soul
Control freak
Cunning

Decisive
Defiant (4)
Dour

Emboldened
Emotional
Enigmatic
Enraged
Expansionist

Frightening (2)
Frosty
Frustrated

Glamorous, shadowy hero
Global menace

Hard man (2)
Hardline (2)
Hawkish
Hollow-cheeked

Imperial
Incapable of calm calculation
Iron man

Karate chopper
KGB professional (3)
Killer

Ladies' Man
Loathsome
Lying brute

Macho (3)
Mad Vlad
Man of mystery (2)
Master of the dark arts
Menacing
Mob boss
Moral backbone of an earthworm

Narcissist (2)
Nimble

Obsessive hatred of democracy
Opportunist

Paranoid
Paranoid intolerance
Paramount political force in Russia
Pariah (2)
Powerful (3)
Powerful as Stalin
Pre-1917 imperial nationalist
Prickly
Pugnacious
Puppet master (2)

Rambling
Rasputin
Reckless

Ruthless (3)

Self-controlled
Shrewd outsider
Spare
Sphinx without a riddle
Spy (2)
Steely (2)
Strait-laced
Strongman (4)
Strutting (2)
Suspicious
Swaggering

Tetchy
Thug
Triumphant
Tsar
Tyrant (2)

Uncompromising (2)
Unlikely sex symbol
Unpleasant
Unrepentant Cold War Warrior

Vindictive
Vlad-father
Vlad joke
Vlad the invader
Vlad the sinister
Vodka tippler
Vulgar

Wooden

Appendix B

British Newspaper Headlines on Proposed Boycott of World Cup 2018 as a Response to the Skripal Poisionings

Foreign Office Suggests UK Might Consider Withdrawing Officials and Dignitaries From World Cup (*Guardian*, 6 March)

We'll Quit World Cup over Russki Spy Terror (*Daily Star*, 6 March)

I'll give Vlad a World Cup Kicking. England set to Quit Tournament over Suspected 'Salisbury Spy' Assassination: Johnson Warning to Putin (*Daily Star*, 7 March)

William's World Cup Visit Could Be in Doubt if Proof of Russian Poison Plot Emerges (*Telegraph*, 7 March)

Will Royals Now Snub World Cup? (*Daily Mail*, 7 March)

Wills & Harry Could Boycott World Cup After Boris Threat (*Daily Mirror*, 7 March)

Duke and Prince Have 'No Plans' to Cheer on England Side in Russia (*Daily Telegraph*, 8 March)

William Planning to Stay Away from World Cup (*Times*, 8 March)

Official: William Will Snub Russia's World Cup as Spy Row Rages (*Daily Mail*, 8 March)

England's WAGs are Set to Snub World Cup (*Daily Mail*, 8 March)

William 'Not Going to the World Cup' (*Express*, 8 March)

Should We Boycott Putin's World Cup? (*Daily Mail*, 9 March)

World Cup Boycott Would Hit Putin Hard (*Daily Mail*, 10 March)

World Kicks Off over the Vladi Footie: Mass Cup Boycott Urged (*Daily Star*, 10 March)

Notes

CHAPTER 1

1. Original copyright by B.W. Huebsch, Inc in 1921.

CHAPTER 2

1. Alex Thomson; interview with the author, London, 29 November 1999.
2. John Simpson; telephone Interview with the author 9 December 1999.
3. Submission to the US Congressional Joint Economic Committee; *Daily Telegraph*, 11 November 1989.
4. The Huw Wheldon Lecture by John Simpson, BBC2 1993.

CHAPTER 3

1. 'Russian Federation: Presidential Election, 26 March 2000. Final Report', Office for Democratic Institutions and Human Rights, OSCE, 19 May 2000: www.osce.org/odihr/elections/russia/16275.
2. 'Russian Federation: Presidential election, 14 March 2004. Final Report', Office for Democratic Institutions and Human Rights, OSCE, 2 June 2004: www.osce.org/odihr/elections/russia/33101.
3. 'OSCE to Boycott Russian Election', BBC News Channel, 7 February 2008.
4. 'Observation of the Presidential Election in the Russian Federation (2008)', PACE, 20 March 2008.
5. 'Russian Federation: Presidential Election, 4 March 2012. Final Report', Office for Democratic Institutions and Human Rights, OSCE, 11 May 2012.
6. 'Russian Federation: Presidential Election, 18 March 2018. Final Report', Office for Democratic Institutions and Human Rights, OSCE, 6 June 2018.
7. Mary Dejevsky: telephone interview with the author, 6 July 2015; cited in Greg McLaughlin, *The War Correspondent* (London: Pluto Press, 2016), 207–8.
8. *Ibid.*

CHAPTER 4

1. See, for example, *The Face of War*, a collection of Gellhorn's war reporting, first published in 1959 and with a third edition published by Granta Books in 1998.

2. Luke Harding's critical reporting of the Putin regime, which he called a 'virtual Mafia state', ended with his deportation in 2011.

3. In October 2015, 8 months after Nemtsov's murder, Seumas Milne took leave from the *Guardian* and was appointed Executive Director of Strategy and Communications for the British Labour Party under its new leader, Jeremy Corbyn. He resigned from the *Guardian* in 2017 to continue in his post on a permanent basis.

4. 'Alexander Litvinenko: Profile of Murdered Russian Spy', BBC online, 21 January 2016: www.bbc.co.uk/news/uk-19647226 (accessed June 2019).

5. 'Russian Spy Poisoning: What We Know So Far', BBC online, 8 October 2018: www.bbc.co.uk/news/uk-43315636 (accessed June 2019).

6. Media reports in the following April revealed that Skripal's two guinea pigs had died from dehydration and neglect while he was in hospital; and that the cat had to be put down due to extreme distress.

7. 'Amesbury Poisoning: What are Novichok Agents and What Do They Do?', BBC online, 5 July 2018: www.bbc.co.uk/news/world-europe-43377698 (accessed June 2019).

8. All headlines are from 12 March 2018 unless noted otherwise.

9. List of World Cup 2018 sponsors cited by Quora: www.quora.com/Who-is-the-official-sponsor-of-the-FIFA-World-Cup (accessed June 2019).

10. Email interview of Mary Dejevsky with the author, 30 August 2019.

CHAPTER 5

1. See 'Russian Federation: What justice for Chechnya's disappeared?', Amnesty International, 23 May 2007; Index No, EUR 46/015/2007.

2. The use of the word black in Russian is a general pejorative for 'outsiders' and is not a reference to racial identity.

3. This alluded to one of the darkest episodes in Soviet history, Stalin's pogrom in the 1930s against the Kulaks, a social class of wealthy Russian peasants, who stood against the Soviet programme of the collectivisation of agricultural land and labour.

4. Director of the Crisis Research Institute, Oxford.

5. The parliamentary sketch has a long tradition in the British press. It goes back to the early eighteenth century and is still a feature in most elite newspapers today. As a form of political critique, it is meant to be satirical in tone and content as part of the role of the newspaper to hold the powerful to account.

6. See, for example, academic studies of the Vietnam War, 1965–1975 (Hallin, 1986); the Falklands War, 1982 (Morrison and Tumber, 1988); the Gulf War, 1991 (Philo and McLaughlin, 1995); the Northern conflict and the peace process (McLaughlin and Miller, 1996; McLaughlin and Baker, 2010 and 2015); the Kosovo conflict (McLaughlin, 2002); the Iraq War 2003 (Tumber and Palmer, 2004).

7. See report by Amnesty International, 'Georgia/Russia: Civilians in the Line of Fire: The Georgia–Russia Conflict', 18 November 2008: www.amnesty. org/en/documents/EUR04/005/2008/en/.

8. Colin Powell interviewed in 'Democracy Threatens', Part Two of the four-part series *Putin, Russia and the West*, BBC2, January 2012.

9. Colin Powell, interviewed in 'War', Part Three of the four-part series *Putin, Russia and the West*, BBC2, February 2012.

10. This case study is a revised and updated version of that presented in Greg McLaughlin, *The War Correspondent*, 2nd edn (London: Pluto Press, 2016), 204–9.

11. The *Daily Mail* was publicly supportive of Hitler's expansionism in Europe up until the invasion of Poland in 1939 and Britain's declaration of war against Germany.

12. See the full post of Ian H. Robertson 'The Danger that Lurks Inside Vladimir Putin's Brain', *Psychology Today*, 17 March 2014, at: www.psychologytoday. com/blog/the-winner-effect/201403/the-danger-lurks-inside-vladimir-putins-brain (accessed March 2015).

13. Al-Nusra Front was also known as Jabhat al-Nusra or Al-Qaeda in Syria/ the Levant.

14. At the time of publication of the article, McFaul was the director of the Freeman Spogli Institute for International Studies at Stanford University and a senior fellow at the Hoover Institution.

15. Mary Devjevsky: email interview with the author, 30 August 2019.

CHAPTER 6

1. 'Obama Ends Missile Defence Shield in Europe', *Guardian*, 17 September 2009: www.theguardian.com/world/2009/sep/17/missile-defence-shield-barack-obama (accessed 2019).

2. 'Secrets, Spies and Useful Idiots', Part 2 of three-part series *Trump/Russia*, Four Corners programme, Australian Broadcasting Corporation, 2018.

3. 'Nuclear Posture Review', US Department of Defense, 2018: https:// media.defense.gov/2018/Feb/02/2001872886/-1/-1/1/2018-NUCLEAR-POSTURE-REVIEW-FINAL-REPORT.PDF (accessed August 2019).

CHAPTER 7

1. Email interview of Mary Dejevsky with the author, 30 August 2019.

2. *Ibid.*

3. *Ibid.*

4. *Ibid.*

References

Aubrey, Crispin (ed.) (1982) *Nukespeak: The Media and the Bomb*. London: Comedia/Minority Press Group.

Bourdieu, Pierre (1972) 'Systems of Education and Systems of Thought' In Michael F.D. Young (ed.), *Knowledge and Control: New Directions for the Sociology of Education*. London: Collier-Macmillan.

Browder, Bill (2015) *Red Notice: How I Became Putin's No. 1 Enemy*. London: Corgi Books.

Chang, Wong Ho (1991) 'Images of the Soviet Union in American Newspapers: A Content Analysis of Three Newspapers'. In Everette E. Dennis, George Gerbner and Yassen N. Zassoursky (eds), *Beyond the Cold War: Soviet and American Media Images*. London: Sage, 65–83.

Chekhov, Anton (1987) *Notebook of Anton Chekhov*. New York: Eco Press.

Chomsky, Noam (1989) *Necessary Illusions*. London: Pluto Press.

Dennis, Everette E., Gerbner, George and Zassoursky, Yassen N. (eds) (1991) *Beyond the Cold War: Soviet and American Media Images*. London: Sage.

Eco, Umberto (2013) *Inventing the Enemy: Essays on Everything*. London: Vintage.

Entman, Robert M. and Rojecki, Andrew (1993) 'Freezing out the Public: Elite and Media framing of the US Anti-Nuclear Movement'. *Political Communication* (10)2: 155–73.

Felshtinsky, Yuri and Litvinenko, Alexander (2002) *Blowing up Russia: Terror from Within*. London: SPI Books.

Fukuyama, Francis (1992) *The End of History and the Last Man*. London: Hamish Hamilton.

Galeotti, Mark (2019) *We Need to Talk About Putin: How the West Gets Him Wrong*. London: Penguin/Random House.

Gellhorn, Martha (1998 [1959]) *The Face of War*, 3rd edn. London: Granta Books.

Gerbner, George (1991) 'The Image of Russians in American Media and the "New Epoch"'. In Everette E. Dennis, George Gerbner and Yassen N. Zassoursky (eds), *Beyond the Cold War: Soviet and American Media Images*. London: Sage, 31–5.

Gessen, Masha (2014) *The Man Without a Face: The Unlikely Rise of Vladimir Putin*. London: Granta Publishing.

Gitlin, Todd (1980) *The Whole World is Watching: The Mass Media in the Making and the Unmaking of the New Left*. Berkeley, CA: University of California Press.

Glasgow University Media Group (GUMG) (1985) *War and Peace News*. Milton Keynes: Open University Press.

Halliday, Julian, Curry Jansen, Sue and Schneider, James (1992) 'Framing the Crisis in Eastern Europe'. In Mark Raboy and Bernard Dagenais (eds), *Media, Crisis and Democracy: Mass Communication and the Disruption of Social Order*. London: Sage, 63–78.

Hallin, Daniel C. (1986) *The 'Uncensored War': The Media and Vietnam*. Berkeley, CA: University of California Press.

Hallin, Daniel C. and Mancini, Paolo (1989) *Friendly Enemies*. Perugia: Perugia Press.

Harding, Luke (2016) *A Very Expensive Poisoning*. London: Guardian Books.

Knightley, Phillip (2004) *The First Casualty: The War Correspondent as Hero and Myth Maker from the Crimea to Iraq*, 3rd edn. Baltimore, MD: Johns Hopkins University Press.

Kovalik, Dan (2017) *The Plot to Scapegoat Russia: How the CIA and the Deep State Have Conspired to Vilify Russia*. New York: Skyhorse Publishing.

Lee Myers, Steven (2015) *The New Tsar: The Rise and Reign of Vladimir Putin*. London: Simon & Schuster.

Lippmann, Walter and Merz, Charles (1920) 'A Test of the News'. *The New Republic*, Vol. 23, Part II, No. 296.

Lucas, Edward (2014) *The New Cold War: Putin's Threat to Russia and the West*. London: Bloomsbury.

Lukosiunas, Marius A. (1991) 'Enemy, Friend, or Competitor? A Content Analysis of the *Christian Science Monitor* and *Izvestia*'. In Everette E. Dennis, George Gerbner and Yassen N. Zassoursky (eds), *Beyond the Cold War: Soviet and American Media Images*. London: Sage, 100–10.

McLaughlin, Greg (1993) 'Coming In from the Cold: British TV Coverage of the East European Revolutions'. In James Aulich and Tim Wilcox (eds), *Europe Without Walls: Art, Posters and Revolution 1989–93*. Manchester: Manchester City Art Galleries, 189–99.

McLaughlin, Greg (1999) 'Refugees, Migrants and the Fall of the Berlin Wall'. In Greg Philo (ed.), *Message Received*. London: Longman, 197–209.

McLaughlin, Greg (2002) 'Rules of Engagement: TV Journalism and NATO's "Faith in Bombing" During the Kosovo Crisis'. *Journalism Studies* (3)2: 257–66.

McLaughlin, Greg (2016) *The War Correspondent*, 2nd edn. London: Pluto Press, 168–9.

McLaughlin, Greg and Baker, Stephen (2010) *The Propaganda of Peace: The Role of Culture and Media the Irish Peace Process*. London: Intellect.

McLaughlin, Greg and Baker, Stephen (2015) *The British Media and Bloody Sunday*. London: Intellect.

McLaughlin, Greg and Miller, David (1996) 'The Media Politics of the Irish Peace Process'. *International Journal Press/Politics* 1(4): 116–34.

McNair, Brian (1988) *Images of the Enemy*. London: Routledge.

Mickiewicz, Ellen (1991) 'Images of America'. In Everette E. Dennis, George Gerbner and Yassen N. Zassoursky (eds), *Beyond the Cold War: Soviet and American Media Images*. London: Sage, 21–30.

Miller, David (2004) 'The Propaganda Machine'. In David Miller (ed.), *Tell Me Lies: Propaganda and Media Distortion in the Attack on Iraq*. London: Pluto Press, 80–99.

Morrison, David and Tumber, Howard (1988) *Journalists at War: The Dynamics of News Reporting During the Falklands War*. London: Sage.

Parenti, Michael (1983) *Inventing Reality: The Politics of the News Media*, 1st edn. New York: St Martin's Press.

Philips Price, Morgan (1997) *Dispatches from the Revolution, Russia 1916–18*, Tania Rose (ed.). London: Pluto Press.

Philo, Greg and McLaughlin, Greg (1995) 'The British Media and the Gulf War'. In Greg Philo (ed.), *The Glasgow Media Group Reader, Vol. 2*. London: Routledge, 146–56.

Politkovskaya, Anna (2001) *A Dirty War: A Russian Reporter in Chechnya*. London: Harvill Press.

Politkovskaya, Anna (2004) *Putin's Russia*. London: Harvill Press.

Politkovskaya, Anna (2007) *Anna Politkovskaya: A Russian Diary*, with Foreword by Jon Snow. London: Harvill Secker.

Pomerantsev, Peter (2015) *Nothing is True and Everything is Possible: Adventures in Modern Russia*. London: Faber & Faber.

Reed, John (1926) *Ten Days That Shook the World*. London: Martin Lawrence.

Richter, Andrei G. (1991) 'Enemy Turned Partner: A Content Analysis of *Newsweek* and *Novoye Vremya*'. In Everette E. Dennis, George Gerbner and Yassen N. Zassoursky (eds), *Beyond the Cold War: Soviet and American Media Images*. London: Sage, 91–9.

Roxburgh, Angus (2013) *The Strongman: Vladimir Putin and the Struggle for Russia*. London: I.B. Tauris.

Rukavishnikov, Vladimir (2008) 'The U.S.–Russian Dispute Over Missile Defense'. *Connections* 7(4): 81–94, www.jstor.org/stable/26323365 (accessed 2019).

Sabey, Ruth (1982) 'Disarming the Disarmers'. In Crispin Aubrey (ed.), *Nukespeak: The Media and the Bomb*. London: Comedia/Minority Press Group, 55–63.

Simpson, John (1990) *Dispatches from the Barricades: An Eyewitness Account of the Revolutions that Shook the World, 1989–90*. London: Hutchinson.

Thompson, Edward (1982) 'Notes on Exterminism, the Last Stage of Civilization'. In *New Left Review* (ed.) *Exterminsim and Cold War*. London: Verso, 1–34.

Trenin, Dimitri (2016) *Should We Fear Russia?* Cambridge: Polity Press.

Tumber, Howard and Palmer, Jeffrey (2004) *Media at War: The Iraq Crisis*. London: Sage.

Unger, Craig (2018) *House of Trump, House of Putin: The Untold Story of Donald Trump and the Russian Mafia*. London: Penguin/Random Press.

Walker, Shaun (2018) *The Long Hangover: Putin's New Russia and the Ghosts of the Past*. Oxford: Oxford University Press.

Zassoursky, Yassen N. (1991) 'Changing Images of the Soviet Union and the United States'. In Everette E. Dennis, George Gerbner and Yassen N. Zassoursky (eds), *Beyond the Cold War: Soviet and American Media Images*. London: Sage, 11–20.

Index